A Canopy in the Desert

OTHER WORKS BY ABBA KOVNER
(in Hebrew only)

NOVEL

Face To Face

POETRY

Until No Light
The Key Sank
Sandy Soil
A Rock Group Plays on Mount Gerizim
The Little Book: Collected and New Poems

A CANOPY IN THE DESERT

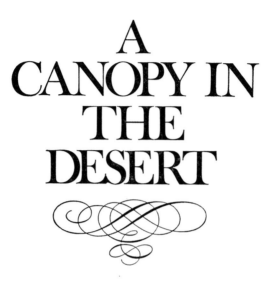

Selected Poems *by*

ABBA KOVNER

Translated from the Hebrew by
SHIRLEY KAUFMAN
with Ruth Adler and Nurit Orchan

University of Pittsburgh Press

ISBN 0–8229–3260–1 (cloth)
ISBN 0–8229–5232–7 (paper)
Copyright © 1973, Shirley Kaufman
All rights reserved
Media Directions Inc., London
Manufactured in the United States of America

From All the Loves was originally published in Hebrew under the title *Mikol Haahavot* (Tel Aviv: Sifriat Poalim, 1965).

My Little Sister was originally published in Hebrew under the title *Aḥoti Ktana* (Tel Aviv: Sifriat Poalim, 1967).

A Parting from the South was originally published in Hebrew under the title *Prida Mehadarom* (Tel Aviv: Sifriat Poalim, 1949).

A Canopy in the Desert was originally published in Hebrew under the title *Ḥupa Bamidbar* (Tel Aviv: Sifriat Poalim, 1970).

The above books copyright © Abba Kovner and Sifriat Poalim, 1970.

The Hebrew poems on pages 2, 16, 74, and 94 are reprinted by permission of the publisher, Sifriat Poalim Ltd., © 1970 Abba Kovner and Sifriat Poalim Ltd.

The English translation of *My Little Sister* was first published in *Abba Kovner and Nelly Sachs: Selected Poems* in the Penguin Modern European Poets series (Harmondsworth, Eng.: Penguin Books, 1971).

Grateful acknowledgment is also made to *Ariel* and to *Midstream*, which published some of the translations from *From All the Loves*.

With what—
with what, little sister,
shall we weave and draw the dream
now?

Abba Kovner, *My Little Sister*

Past and present and future are not disjoin'd but join'd. The greatest poet forms the consistence of what is to be, from what has been and is. He drags the dead out of their coffins and stands them again on their feet. He says to the past, "Rise and walk before me that I may realize you."

Walt Whitman, Preface to *Leaves of Grass*

Contents

Foreword

The hope of the International Poetry Forum is to be no less international than poetry itself. To be sure, such a hope invites certain practical limitations. While poetry has the destiny of speaking to all men at all times, the International Poetry Forum concerns itself with bringing particular poets into contact with as many people as possible right now. While poetry speaks ultimately from and to the common nationality of flesh and blood, the International Poetry Forum attempts in a proximate way to permit poets of different nationalities and alphabets to have their work known and understood by people of nationalities and alphabets other than their own.

To help achieve this goal the International Poetry Forum has initiated a series of foreign selections. These selections provide for the publication of American translations of some of the works of foreign poets and the distribution of such books throughout the United States, Europe, and the poets' homelands.

The Israeli Selection is the fourth in this series, the first three having been the Turkish Selection (*Selected Poems*) to Fazıl Hüsnü Dağlarca in 1969, the Syria-Lebanon Selection (*The Blood of Adonis*) to Adonis (Ali Ahmed Said) in 1971, and the Swedish Selection (*Windows and Stones*) to Tomas Tranströmer in 1972.

SAMUEL HAZO

Acknowledgments

These translations could not have been made without the collaboration of two Israelis: Nurit Orchan, for *My Little Sister*, and Ruth Adler, for the other translations.

For valuable suggestions in the translation of *My Little Sister*, I wish to acknowledge the counsel of Dr. Leib Schapiro, Chana Bloch, and Robert Alter, Professor of Hebrew and Comparative Literature at the University of California, Berkeley. Professor Alter also prepared the notes for *My Little Sister*.

Further thanks are due to Professor Benjamin Hrushovski of Tel-Aviv University, whose assistance in the interpretation of the Hebrew texts of *A Parting from the South* and *A Canopy in the Desert*, was invaluable; to Ora Mayrose; and to Dan Laor of the Hebrew University, Jerusalem. Dan Laor prepared the notes for these two works.

I am grateful also to Mary Clemmey for her encouragement, to Professor Dan Miron and T. Carmi who read and corrected the translation of *My Little Sister*, and to Dov Vardi for his detailed suggestions regarding *A Canopy in the Desert*. Mark Linenthal, Professor of English and Creative Writing and Director of the Poetry Center at State University of California at San Francisco, was a helpful critic of the poetry in English.

And, finally, I wish to thank the poet himself for his thoughtful and illuminating correspondence. I was privileged to make the final corrections on the manuscript of *My Little Sister* with Abba Kovner on his kibbutz in Israel; he interpreted and read the rest of the manuscript with me in San Francisco.

S.K.

Introduction

Reading his poems in Hebrew while on tour through the United States in January 1972, Abba Kovner told his audience: "When I write I am like a man praying."

He went on: "I inherited many things from my ancestors. One is the teaching that a man should not say his own prayer before the prayer of his community. . . . But the community in which I pray and say my poems is half alive and half dead. Who are the living and who are the dead? I don't know how to answer this question. But I believe there is one place in the world without cemeteries. This is the place of poetry. And because of this belief, I stand here before you."

And now the poems of Abba Kovner, standing before us in translation, ask the same question: Who are the living and who are the dead?

*

In *My Little Sister*, the poet asks:

> How mourn a city
> whose people are dead and whose dead are alive
> in the heart.

The city was Vilna, capital of Lithuania, center of Jewish culture and creativity. The year was 1941. The Germans had occupied a strip of Russian territory five hundred miles deep and one thousand miles long from the Baltic to the Black Sea. Behind this strip nearly six million Jews were caught, with German armies in the rear. From June to November the Nazis took forty-seven thousand Jews out of Vilna. They said they were taking them to a labor camp at Ponar; the rest, who were locked behind the gates of the ghetto, would go when the camp and its factories could absorb them.

In November a young girl crawled up over the thousands of bodies in the pits at Ponar and made her way twenty miles through a frozen forest back to the Vilna ghetto. No one could believe her story, forty thousand Jews dead in a ditch. But Abba Kovner listened and believed. He was twenty-two years old. He wrote the first Jewish call to arms in the Vilna ghetto, a pathetic call since there was no way to get guns or ammunition.

Two years later the Jews of Vilna, like the Jews in more than fifty other ghettos in Eastern Europe, starved, butchered, terrorized by incredible savagery, saw nothing ahead but death and madness. Abba Kovner became the leader of their fighting resistance, the United Partisan Organization. He and a few others, strong enough to lead with him, began to take whoever could walk or crawl out of the Vilna ghetto through the sewers into the forests. Perhaps in the forests they could find a way to defend themselves.

To discourage escape attempts, the Germans introduced "collective responsibility," making whole families and groups responsible for the escape of a single individual. The ghetto fighters faced desperate moral and personal questions. If they left the ghetto to go to the forests, they endangered the lives of their families. Besides, they were torn by the choice of whether to go to the forests and die fighting (few hoped to survive) or to stay with those who could not escape and share their fate within the walls of the ghetto. It was agonizing to leave one's family, even knowing that remaining with them could not save their lives. In *A Canopy in the Desert* we hear Kovner's remembering cry: "I wanted to choose" (17). He cannot even say it in words; he puts it in Morse code. In a world that had lost meaning, Abba Kovner, and others like him, had to find the courage to accept full responsibility for his decision. His religion taught him that the world is good and life is precious, but history taught him that the world is evil and that life is expendable.

In his lifetime he has witnessed the Nazi Holocaust, the Russian purges, Israel's struggle to become a nation again and to exist.

He has witnessed the free nations of the world holding conferences on refugees, issuing refined statements of concern and outrage, and doing nothing. He has witnessed his people, his own family, shoveled into mass graves, gassed, and burned alive. He has witnessed the sinking of shiploads of survivors in the waters of the Mediterranean because no land would take them. But the central fact in Kovner's life is his confrontation with the half-dead, half-crazed girl from the mass grave at Ponar. Her face haunts every line he writes. We never see her eyes, her features—we never know her name. But we hear her voice. And the silence after the voice.

*

Abba Kovner was born in 1918 in the Crimea (Sebastopol) where his father had gone from a town near Vilna on his way to Palestine. The family was caught there, unable to leave when World War I broke out. After the war his family settled in Vilna, where he attended a Hebrew high school and joined Hashomer Hatzair, the Zionist Socialist youth movement.

After the German occupation and his activity in the Partisans, Kovner embarked for Palestine in 1947 as an illegal immigrant. He was caught by the British while still aboard ship, was imprisoned in Cairo, and was finally transferred to a Jerusalem prison from which the Haganah (Jewish underground army of Palestine) succeeded in freeing him. He became a member of Kibbutz Ein Haḥoresh, and lives there today with his wife and two children. During the Israeli War of Independence in 1948, he was cultural officer of the Givati Brigade on the southern front.

His work includes a novel about the War of Independence; several collections which he edited of writings by Partisans, survivors of the Holocaust, and Israeli children living in border settlements during the Six-Day War; and nine volumes of poetry, all but two of which are lyric-dramatic book-length poems which fuse personal and historical material.

*

Abba Kovner was awarded the highest literary prize in Israel in 1970, the Israel Prize in Literature, and in 1971 he received the International Remembrance Award for literature relating to the Holocaust and its aftermath. Today he is one of the most acclaimed of all poets in Israel. But his vision, intensely Jewish and Israeli, is, above all, human. Because Abba Kovner is tied to his own history, no history is alien to him. When he confronts the pain and guilt of Jewish suffering, he confronts the pain and guilt of all of us. For what have we done to change the world?

It is remarkable that poets like Kovner, in a country of concentration camp survivors, in a state surrounded by enemies, in a large military establishment always on the brink of war, fearing for their own sons' lives in battles which go on and on, avoid the pitfalls of chauvinism or self-pity. But it is their peculiar condition to be linked to three thousand years of history through their own language and landscape. The past is as powerful as the present, and they are forced to examine it all. The reality of their heritage —the Bible, the literature surrounding the Bible, and the land— validates the experience of their own time.

Stephen Spender, in his introduction to the British edition of Kovner's *My Little Sister*, writes:

> In the Old Testament poetry is not an end in itself but the realization in language of a vision of life as old as the nation's history. Thus the traditional Jewish poet/prophet does not write simply as an individual artist expressing his exceptional sensibility for the benefit of other individuals. Instead, he is the voice of the people, a people for whom nationhood is religion and the individual but a fraction of the nation's millennial consciousness. His purposes are didactic and mystical, not aesthetic. (*Abba Kovner and Nelly Sachs: Selected Poems*)

His purposes. Yes. But the result is aesthetic as well. For life cannot be truly re-created except through art. Kovner's life, without art, would be reduced to heaps of shoes and dead ashes. But his ashes "sprout" in the desert. The sparks are all around us. We breathe the acrid smoke, and our eyes sting. Kovner has said: "For me poetry is not merely an ecstatic experience, but an enduring attempt to turn ashes into an eternal light."

In one sweep he gathers the past and the future, the human and superhuman, national and total space. His occasional obscurity is not from the poetry's complexity but from the wilderness he explores, the mystery of human tragedy. He presses into it with words and the breathing between words, and we must follow into his own darkness. Sometimes there are only bones along the way, and we must put the flesh around them. Sometimes it is like walking through a long tunnel. If we keep going—to the end—we will come out into the light.

There are times when not to understand, or not to understand completely, is more important, more instant, more significant, than total comprehension. Ambiguity and mist are both qualities that help turn life into art. This is how Kovner writes. And this is how we must read him.

*

Hebrew is one of the oldest languages on earth. The earliest example of written Hebrew (on the calendar of Gezer, a limestone tablet found eighteen miles north of Jerusalem) was written in Canaanite script some three thousand years ago. The language as it is spoken in the streets of Israel today is essentially the ancient Hebrew of the Bible, together with the Talmud and Midrash, the rabbinic commentaries, exposition, and implementation of the Bible, which were written over a period of almost a thousand years. Used only as a sacred and scholarly language for centuries, Hebrew was revived as a modern language for speaking and nonreligious writing less than a hundred years ago. New words had to be derived from old forms, but its characteristic grammar and vocabulary (a mere 8,000 words!) are still from the Bible. Every Hebrew sentence is composed of words that echo the ancient past. Each word has a mythic as well as a present reality.

When Kovner writes in *My Little Sister, "aḥoti kala"* (my sister-bride), the words echo like music from the Song of Songs (4:9 and 5:1). When he writes in that same book and also in *A Canopy in the Desert*, "*harey at*" (behold you), every reader of Hebrew knows these are the first two words spoken by the Jewish bridegroom during the most sacred moment of the marriage ceremony, and he is able to fill in the rest of the phrase.

The translator of Hebrew poetry and his non-Hebrew-speaking reader face unfortunate obstacles. We are no longer familiar with the Bible in English, let alone in Hebrew. So how is it possible for a reader unacquainted with the words of Scripture in their original context, and unfamiliar with the Talmudic and other traditional literature, to grasp the richness of these allusions? They are simply lost.

A few more examples will underline the problem. In the poem titled "Opening" from *A Parting from the South*, the young soldiers hear "Only the surge of *mighty waters* and an ancient voice." The Hebrew for "mighty waters," *mayim adirim*, is a phrase from Moses' victory song (Exod. 15:10) after crossing the Red Sea. If we recognize this, we are immediately taken back to that time, and we join it to the present battle.

In *A Canopy in the Desert* (18), the wanderer meets someone who says to him:

> please be welcome under the shadow
> of my sand.

Betsel ḥolotay (under the shadow of my sand) echoes *betsel korati* (under the shadow of my roof) from Gen. 19:8. This is Lot speaking to the men of Sodom who surrounded his house while he was protecting the angels of God who had come to warn him of the city's impending destruction. If we recognize the voice of Lot in this phrase, the speaker's next reference to being drunk on wine immediately makes sense. For after the family escaped from Sodom, Lot's daughters made him drunk (in order to sleep with him). As if a match were suddenly struck to reveal a face—there he is! The drunk man reels into the desert and is saved from his burning city.

There are allusions like this throughout Kovner's poetry, throughout all poetry in Hebrew. It would help to know that the whale that "throws him up on the shore / glistening" in *A Canopy in the Desert* (86) is Jonah's whale, and also that coming from the whale means, according to rabbinic tradition, emerging from exile.

It would help to know the wealth of associations which one word like "ladder" can evoke for the informed Hebrew reader. Kovner understands gematria, a method of disclosing the hidden meaning of a biblical or other text by figuring the numerical equivalents of the Hebrew letters (every Hebrew letter has its corresponding number). This form of interpretation is used mainly in the Talmudic-Midrashic and Cabalistic (mystical) literature. Thus, the ladder Jacob saw in his dream, reaching from earth to heaven, refers to Sinai, since the numerical value of *sulam* (ladder) is 130, the same numerical value as that of *Sinai*. This means that the Torah (the Law and the teachings) revealed at Sinai is the ladder which leads from earth to heaven.

Now consider the beautiful legend attributed to Rabbi Mena-hem-Mendl of Kotsk. He told his disciples:

> The souls descended from the realms of Heaven to earth on a ladder. Then the ladder was taken away. Now up there they are calling the souls home. Some do not budge from the spot, for how can one get to Heaven without a ladder? Others leap and fall, and leap again and give up. But there are those who know very well that they cannot make it, but try and try over and over again until God catches hold of them and pulls them up. (Martin Buber, *Tales of the Hasidim*)

Then when we read the word *ladder* in *My Little Sister*, as in the passage about the convent where she is hidden

A ladder leans to a wall,

as in a section describing the Dominican nuns

[xix]

> Night after night
> the Sisters breathe hard in their beds
> as if raised on a ladder,

and as their god

> comes down
> on a ladder of thorns,

or when we read in *A Canopy in the Desert* that Dido, the boy who
will grow up to crash as an Israeli pilot in the Six-Day War, has
crooked legs that

> explore
> blind
> the wooden ladder,   (36)

then we know the richness of one word.

*

If we do not know the Bible, and the words cannot resound for
us in the original context, if we do not know all the details of
Kovner's own life, so that we cannot use these private experiences
to enlarge our understanding of his historical and personal poems,
the poetry, even without this special knowledge, can speak to us.
For Kovner's language and symbolism are not exclusively private,
although I have emphasized that aspect. *Ashes, gold teeth, walls,
bugged thickets* belong to a world we recognize, from the Nazi
death camps to Hiroshima to Mylai. Kovner's experience is
strongly personal, but our perception of it makes it universal.

Kovner speaks in what T. S. Eliot has called "the three voices of
poetry." We hear the voice of the poet talking to himself, talking
to us, and talking through the characters he creates. Frequently he
shifts the voices. The poet switches from first to second to third
person. We, you, I, she—they all become one. And these voices
transcend the limits of time. They speak from the ancient past,
the immediate yesterday, even the future.

In many passages Kovner continues the ancient tradition of the

[xx]

piyut or liturgical poem, most notably in *My Little Sister* (41) (see Kovner's own comments on this in the Appendix). The original *piyut* was a metrical composition inspired by synagogue services. This prayer-poem, and there were tens of thousands of them, borrowed language and meters from the Scriptures and drew its material from the biblical commentaries of the Midrash and Talmud. The *piyut*, marked by brevity, used imagery, many variations of rhyme, and acrostics. The music of the sounds played an important part in tuning the mind of the reader to the message. In Kovner's very contemporary poetry, we can recognize the *piyut*.

In many poems he uses an interesting graphic technique, splitting the verse into columns and masses for emphasis. There is a certain affinity here, as well as in sound and word choice, to the forms of medieval Hebrew poetry. "Many Years. A New Freeway," the first poem in this collection, is a good example of the technique.

Kovner's poetry places an obligation on its translator, beyond the meaning of the words themselves, to test the sound of the language, the pulse of the rhythm, the music of the internal rhymes. Many sections in *A Parting from the South* are end-rhymed, and I have attempted, not as successfully as I would like, to duplicate some of this in English.

Kovner's technical skill—the effects he creates by rhyme, assonance, rhythm, dramatic shifts in diction, unusual syntax—is impressive. It is almost impossible to attain these effects in English and preserve the essential meaning.

*

In this volume there are some selections of single poems from *From All the Loves*, a slightly abridged version of *A Parting from the South*, and the complete texts of *My Little Sister* and *A Canopy in the Desert*. It will be clear, at the end, that Kovner is writing one poem and that his poem (unlike Eugene O'Neill's autobiographical play) is a long night's journey into day. Like the Genesis story of creation, he is moving from chaos to order, or the possibility of order, as at the end of *A Canopy in the Desert*:

> I quietly try to rebuild
> a city, transparent. To sail confused houses
> in two-way streets. To give them back
> their faces, to arrange
> rotating crops, to let the sea
> break through into the small square
> rooms and wash the frost flowers
> and sand stripes alternately from the windows
> like an old-fashioned devoted servant. Already
>
> there is a road.
> A road sign.
> It's really possible to go. (96)

The struggle to survive is eternal and timeless. Kovner knows it in everything he writes. Past, present, future collide in each moment of awareness. We kill so that we will not be killed. We die so that others will not die. "You would come / in order to go without coming back," he hears the woman's voice speaking to him and in him at the edge of the desert. And there seems to be no end to this.

"The next ones go, here they go / after me," the young soldier says in *A Parting from the South*. Even in the arms of his beloved, rising "from the heat of [her] body," he knows that this battle, this war, every battle, every war solves nothing.

The battle was won, but *A Parting from the South* is about loss, not victory—and not only the loss of Dambam, who fell on the southern front in the Israeli War of Independence. It is about the loss of all those who went before him, of all who will follow after:

> They march behind us. . . .
> A step falls in each step. . . .
> A shadow clutches its shadow. . . .

The shadows of family, of friends in the ghetto of Vilna, of six million Jews, of all the martyrs of history.

> My shadows, shadows. No use to walk behind us!

The shadow of *My Little Sister* also appears in *A Parting from the South*, though the former was written almost twenty years later. On one level, this is the story of a child hidden in a Catholic convent to save her life while the Nazis destroy her world outside the convent walls. But the enormity of the Holocaust cannot be realized in individual tragedy. How many little sisters were there who could not be saved? The mind staggers before so much suffering. How could it have happened? In the end it is too much even to comprehend. Who are the living? Who are the dead?

In *A Canopy in the Desert* we meet Dambam, the dead soldier of *A Parting from the South*, and the little sister again. It is Kovner's most remarkable achievement so far, and its complexity needs some introduction, if only as a way of reading beyond what seems to be the narrative.

A Canopy in the Desert (*Ḥupa Bamidbar*) is about a strange journey and a wedding which does not happen. The *ḥupa* is a wedding canopy, still used in Jewish marriages, to remind us of the tent ceremony in biblical times when the veiled bride was brought into the groom's tent (Gen. 24:67). The *midbar* is the desert where Moses led 600,000 Hebrew slaves out of Egypt. It is the desert at the foot of Mount Sinai where Moses made his Covenant with God, a Covenant which enslaved his people in a new way. It is the desert where the newly created state of Israel fought three wars for its right to exist. It is the desert where the very shapes of stone and granite columns seem to kneel before God in the blazing sun, but where man keeps coming back to struggle against man, to struggle against God.

> ... too weak to wipe out
> our arrogant stubbornness!   (20)

And it is the desert with its vast emptiness of sand, canyons, and dry wadis through which the memory of every disaster pours. We find ourselves in a real yet imagined landscape, then and now, where things are both familiar and strange—and where distinctions between inner and outer, life and death, past and present whirl together in the sand. Over and over, the sand of this eternal desert tells man he is alien, he does not belong here:

> Our footsteps are gone

and again in *A Parting from the South*:

> ... his feet trace-and-do-not-trace

and then in *A Canopy in the Desert* (19):

> ... Footsteps in the canyon
> simply left no trace.

But he returns and returns.

Who are the living and who are the dead? The live narrator of the poem, the poet-wanderer, embodies all of the dead who have wandered in the Vilna ghetto, the forests of the Partisans, and the Sinai desert, real or imagined (and therefore perhaps more real), before him. And the dead speak in him and to him and through him to us with voices which are alive, with memories we can never lose or bury.

The voices he hears and the men he meets in the desert come from the dead, but in another sense they are the external and visible consciousness of the narrator-poet-wanderer himself. For he is really alone with his consciousness in this vast space of sand and ashes.

Why does he keep hearing these voices? Why can't he lose these memories? They come out of what he regards as the three most significant events in Jewish history: the Covenant at Sinai, the Holocaust, and the re-creation of the Jewish state in Israel.

When Moses accepted the Torah at Mount Sinai, the people vowed to live by it:

> Behold, I set before you this day a blessing and a curse: the blessing,
> if ye shall hearken unto the commandments of the Lord your God,
> which I command you this day; and the curse, if ye shall not hearken

unto the commandments of the Lord your God, but turn aside out
of the way which I command you this day. (Deut. 11:26–28)

What diabolic injunction was it they accepted at Sinai? Thou
shalt not murder? And for what were they chosen? Kovner faces
one of the greatest of all blasphemies—we revere a law in theory
and repudiate it in practice. In *A Canopy in the Desert* he goes
into the wilderness to search for a new Revelation, or simply to
find the old one again and make it work:

> . . . I came
> because I came to inherit.   (41)

And, as in the beginning of *A Parting from the South*, he again
stares at the death of soldiers and hears the strange, ancient echoes
of the Sinai desert. Once again he is cut off from the outside world
and hears the lost voices of his past. Once again there is a sense of
mirage in which the burning ghetto and the burning desert are
confused and shifting.

How does a man live who must face war over and over wherever
he goes? In a world that is destructible, he must identify himself
with the indestructible. He must marry the desert! But this, too, is
denied him as a way to find peace. For this desert is, after all, not
only the wilderness of Moses where a people of rescued slaves was
forged into a nation with a divine Covenant and an extraordinary
sense of common destiny. It is also a place in the real world of the
twentieth century with its own political and historical significance.

In the Bible the prophet Hosea (2:21) saw Israel—its land, its
people—as the bride of God: "I will betroth thee unto Me forever."
Kovner's poet-narrator-wanderer, the living–the dead, seeks to wed
the desert. But in the end the desert is wedded only to God.

*

A Canopy in the Desert is divided into twelve *gates*, an archaic
use of the Hebrew word *sha'ar*, which used to introduce books—a
first page, a first chapter. *Sha'ar* is filled with associations in He-

brew, reminding us of Exod. 20:10 ("the stranger within thy gates") and the entrance to the courts of Kings. The double usage of the Hebrew word, as a way into books as well as into walled cities, has a special significance for Jews, who traditionally believed that when a man took a book in his hand he was like a pilgrim at the gates of a new city, expecting a revelation—knowledge, Torah, God. The historic development of the meaning of *sha'ar*, in a sense, followed Jewish history. When the gates of the Temple were destroyed and the earthly Jerusalem was gone, the gates were believed to ascend to the heavenly Jerusalem, becoming the gates of heaven and the gates of prayer. Kovner hears all these meanings in the word *sha'ar*, and turns to a place where a gate—any gate—may open for him. Nor can he forget what was said in the Talmud: "From the day on which the Temple was destroyed the gates of prayer have been closed, as it says, *Yea, when I cry and call for help He shutteth out my prayer.* But though the gates of prayer are closed, the gates of weeping are not closed" (Berakoth, 32).

Following is a brief outline of each "gate" to serve as a guide to *A Canopy in the Desert*:

First Gate

The wanderer encounters three settlements on the edge of the desert: an Israeli "development town" (for new immigrants), ruins of the ancient Nabataean settlement in Avdat, and an Arab village located in the ancient place of Grar, where signs of destruction from the war are still visible. These three settlements are described in different poetic styles, which point up the changing perspective of the wanderer. The people who live in the new town seem like ghosts, and the destroyed cities of Avdat and Grar seem alive.

Second Gate

A woman's voice is heard when the wanderer says to her: "you were privileged not to know / a taste of return" (10). Suddenly we hear the little sister who (in *My Little Sister*) was "not privileged to be condemned to death" and, finally, "not privileged to see / the light of the day!" And it is also the voice of Shlomit from *A Parting from the South* who would like to safeguard Dambam on their last night together. The conflict between the duty of love and life as duty returns again and again while the voice of the beloved pours out with the sand which flows through her fingers. The voice of the man returns like an echo from the red granite stones.

Third Gate

The wanderer meets a strange figure who will appear again later in the journey, a drunkard, crazed or sunstruck in the desert. It seems the drunkard is every survivor of Sodom in search of a new life. He is the wanderer's other voice, the man who chooses the burning sun of the desert instead of the city of refuge.

Fourth Day of the Week

(What happened to this gate? Has it disappeared like the dead? "Maybe we forgot to count the gates / we carried from town," the wanderer says [41].) The wanderer meets a balloon man, and this experience stays with him until the last encounter in the eleventh gate. The balloon man waves his empty dreams, the inflated hopes of all the young men dead in war. What can you do with dreams when the boys who dreamed them are gone? Fill them with air? Plant them in sand? Sell them to strangers? But he still wants them to grow—to be trees. Let *their* dreams expand and fly up with *your* dreams.

Fifth Gate

We meet Dido/Dambam as a child, longing to own a pilot's watch. The balloon man tells about Dido's childhood as if he had lived beside him all those years. And there are ominous hints of death.

Sixth Gate

Dido has grown up. We hear the pilot's voice before his plane crashes. The journey continues in a huge storm and the morning after. There is danger and risk in looking beyond what can be seen: "How the view opens up at me!" (37). The horizon enlarges, and into that space the desert flows—the space of personal and collective memory.

Seventh Gate

During the Six-Day War, an Egyptian dies in battle in the Valley of Nakhl, a dry riverbed in the middle of the Sinai desert where one of the fiercest battles took place. The wanderer finds this man's unsent letters scattered by the wind, page by page. And farther on, he finds his abandoned shoes and coat. At the end of this section, the wanderer himself gives voice to the Egyptian's thoughts, as if he were completing the letters for the dead man.

Eighth Gate

In contrast to the spiritual faith of the enemy who appeared in God's image in the preceding gate stands the earthly evidence of faith in man's image. The wanderer comes to the foot of Mount Sinai, the mountain of the giving of the Law. But between him and the mountain of God "There's nothing / there. Nothing. Except what / cannot be reached / in the light" (54). Another God stands in the shape of the wall of St. Catherine's Monastery, which is a symbol for *realization.* Here is the historical dialogue between Christianity as realization or fulfillment and Judaism as expectation, whose tragic shadow stretches all through *My Little Sister* (the "Sisters" embody the realization, and the little sister, in her terrible catastrophe, remains as an endless expectation). It appears now in the sharp contrast between the stone steps carved by the monks to the top of the mountain (exactly 3,000!) and the metaphysical ladder of Israel which is Jacob's ladder.

Ninth Gate

The Mitla Pass, scene of the most violent battles in 1956 and 1967, stands not too far from Mount Sinai ("Thou shalt not murder"). One against the other. In this geographic, historic, and moral framework, a merciless and complex judicial process takes place between the wanderer and his own voice. Sun-crazed now, he confronts a situation of guilt and puts himself on trial. The accumulated confrontations with death—the pilot, the Egyptian, the memories of the ghetto and the Partisans, together with his frustration at Mount Sinai ("the gate is transparent / and locked" [55])—are finally more than he can bear. The breaking of the commandment over and over again. Even the future is filled with forebodings of murder. But the witnesses are always too late. And he must defend himself alone.

Tenth Gate

A Canopy in the Desert—this is the bridal canopy hallowed by tradition. The wanderer-poet-narrator-survivor-of-Vilna becomes the bridegroom. He is one man, and he is all of Israel (the poem assumes another dimension) coming to claim his bride—the desert. Love of woman, love of land—the erotic feeling of this section is the profound expression of an authentic relationship, because, as Kovner has stated: "Love means constant expectation." The guests appear in the image of Israeli soldiers, alive in the memory of the narrator, but dead—"name piled on name"—after the battles in the desert.

Eleventh Gate

Dambam reveals his identity, the pilot killed in the Six-Day War. He is the second Dambam to die (the first was the soldier in *A Parting from the South*). And the balloon man turns out to be his father, that soldier from the earlier book, killed in the War of Independence. The long dead confronts the newly dead, a strange and tragic meeting. There can be no peace, no rest in a heritage like this. Confronted with the death of the second Dambam, the balloons become even more empty. And he has more than he knows what to do with now, after so many wars. At the end he offers to sell a dozen for the price of two. Beyond the dramatic situation of the encounter between father and son—who rise from the real place, death, in order to meet in a dream place—the image of the balloon man has an existence of its own, since he embodies *life*—as poetry—and his impact seems the most vital and intense of all the figures who exist in this desert.

A Returned Gate

Is this the gate that was missing on the fourth day? The protagonist, leaving the dead who haunt the desert, even as they all become part of him, goes back to the woman—the voice he heard in the second gate. She seems to be almost alive. She is the sister-bride, more real now than the fantasied desert-bride. She will open for him "in a set time."

Twelfth Gate

The drunkard again. And an attempt to return to life, to sanity, to the real world. But only the dead know their time runs out. Even in the real world, among the living, the wanderer carries his little sister on his back. The poet's question hovers over the end of the twelfth gate and, indeed, over the entire book: Is there not really another *order* besides the existing human order? Is it possible to break through the chaos of the existing order—to another beginning?

*

Kovner's "Jewish" poetry belongs to all of us. His concerns transcend the limits of one people. The central predicament of his poems is not national, but metaphysical and moral. Who are the living and who are the dead? How do we remain human in a world that is inhuman?

Kovner's terrible confrontation with the paradox of belonging

to a people who proclaimed peace as an ideal for mankind, who summoned nations to "beat their swords into plowshares" and "learn war no more"—and then had to learn how to fight and kill in order to survive—his confrontation with the paradox of commitment, of courage, of what he thinks is *right*—of existence itself—gives him no peace.

"With blood and darkness the poem is written, should be written," stated Pablo Neruda when he received the Nobel Prize in Literature. And ten years earlier, in 1960, in his acceptance speech for the award of the same prize for literature, St. John Perse concluded: "It is enough for the poet to be the guilty conscience of his time."

This might be Abba Kovner's own summary of his work (from *A Canopy in the Desert*):

> The best way, my friend,
> leads to a sea to a desert
> to an odor of salt and rain an odor of stone scorched by the sun
> a taste of ore of iron and blood
> to a place from which there is no way
> except for the ones who go, my boy.   (95)

SHIRLEY KAUFMAN

San Francisco
1972

TRANSCRIPTION NOTE

Where Hebrew words have been rendered into English in this volume, Haim Blanc's phonetic transcription of contemporary Israeli Hebrew has been used. However, geographic place names, such as *Sinai*, and well-known Jewish ritual terms, such as *hallah*, are given in their long-accepted English spellings. Some words, like *Cushite*, are transcribed according to their spelling in the English Bible.

Following is a table of the essentials of Israeli pronunciation necessary to this volume:

Symbol	*Equivalent*
ḥ	German Ba*ch*, Spanish *j*unta
r	French *r*at, Spanish to*r*o
ts	ca*ts*
a	f*a*ther
e	b*e*t
i	mach*i*ne
o	sh*o*re
u	tr*u*e
ay	m*y*
ey	gr*ay*

SELECTIONS

FROM

FROM ALL THE LOVES

(*Mikol Haahavot*)

1965

שָׁנִים רַבּוֹת. אוֹטוֹסְטְרָדָה חֲדָשָׁה

אֶת הָאוֹרוֹת הֶחֱלִיפוּ לְצָהֹב: שְׂדֵרָה הָיְתָה בִּמְקוֹם הַפְּנָסִים
בְּמֵאָה עֶשְׂרִים קִילוֹמֶטֶר־לְשָׁעָה גַּם הַתַּמְרוּרִים מְפַנִּים לְךָ
מָקוֹם בְּהַעֲרָצָה   אֲנִי אוֹהֵב אֶת הָעִיר הַלֵּילִית שֶׁרָצָה
לִקְרָאתִי כְּמִנִּפַת קַרְנָבָל זַרְחָנִית   בַּגֶּשֶׁם
עֶשְׂרִים שָׁנָה יוֹרֵד שָׁם גֶּשֶׁם   הַגֶּשֶׁם
סוֹבֵב אֶת פָּנֶיךָ פָּנַיִךְ צָפִים שָׁם   בַּגֶּשֶׁם

אֲנִי מַבִּיט בְּאֶצְבְּעוֹתַי הָאוֹחֲזוֹת בַּהֶגֶה   אֲנִי רוֹאֶה
אֶת צִפָּרְנֵי שֶׁמַּכְחִילוֹת מִקֹּר אֲנִי רוֹאֶה אֶת שְׁנַיִךְ
הַקְּטַנּוֹת בָּאוֹר הַצָּהֹב אַחַר כָּל הַשָּׁנִים הָרַבּוֹת
הָאֵלֶּה וַאֲנִי אוֹהֵב אַהֲבָה עַזָּה אֶת הָעִיר
הַזֹּרָה הָעוֹלָה חֲרִישִׁית אֶת הַכְּבִישׁ
הַנִּגְרָע בְּעֵינַיִם קְמוּת אֶת
מִלְמוּל הַמַּגְבִּים עַל
שִׁמְשַׁת הַמְּכוֹנִית אֶת
אוֹר הַפְלוּאוֹרֶסְצֶנְט
שֶׁחוֹזֵר וְזוֹרֶה
אֶת טִפּוֹת
פָּנֶיךָ
בַּגֶּשֶׁם

[2]

MANY YEARS. A NEW FREEWAY

The lights have been changed to yellow: This was a road with
trees. At 80 miles per hour even traffic signs clear the way
for you with admiration.   I love this city-of-night running
to me like a luminous carnival fan   in rain
for twenty years rain falling there   the rain
circles your face your face floating   in rain

I see my fingers on the steering wheel   I watch
   my fingernails turn blue from the cold   I see your small
         teeth in the yellow light after all these years
            and with a fierce love I love this strange
               city rising quietly. The glazed eyes
               of this captive highway the
                  mumble of wiper against
                     the car's windshield
                     fluorescent   light
                     coming back to
                     scatter drops
                     of your face
                     in   the   rain

THE SCIENTISTS ARE WRONG

Scientists are wrong. The universe was not created
billions of years ago.
It seems to me the universe is created every day.

Scientists are wrong to claim
the universe was created from one primordial
substance.
It seems to me the world is created every day
from various substances with nothing in common.
Only the relative proportion of their masses,
like the elements of sorrow and hope,
make them companions
and curbstones. I'm sorry

that I have to get up, in all modesty, and disagree
with what is so sure and recognized by experts:
that there's no speed faster than the speed of light,
when I and my lighted flesh
just noticed something else right here—
whose speed is even greater than the speed of light
and which also returns,
though not in a straight line, because of the curve of the universe
or because of the innocence of God.

And if we connect all this to an equation, according to the rules,
    maybe
it will make sense that I refuse to believe that her voice
and everything I always cherished
and everything so real and suddenly
lost,
is actually lost forever.

WHAT'S NOT IN THE HEART

1

I do not hold a mirage in my hand—
my shirt's in my hand. The plain filled
with my wheat. All of it. Soaked by dew
flat at my feet. Its beauty simply
turns each image pale. The returning heron
and the apple garden. Sun
plucks at my shoulders like my daughter's fingers.
And this day
recalling soon
the odor of harvest:
this morning (I say to myself)
even in the burned forest the bird
has come back to sing.

2

Useless. I try now to understand that what happened
happened. We declared two minutes of silence
so silence would not grow in the windows
of our homes. And no way out, my brother.
The world does not stay on the cry
of night. On one
with anything in his heart, because
what's in the heart is nothing. Because
the living live by the will of those who go
where
they were not willing to go.

Useless: I try now to define your being—

word-shadows! Only your returning shadow
exists. My hands will never
touch you. Your coffin
never leaves my shoulders.

WHEN I FIRST HUNG IT

When I first hung my father's portrait
                    (in charcoal, black and white)
my heart cried delight.
When you put your lips on my mouth
                    (forever forever forever)
oceans pulled back, my dear.
When Barcelona stood in flames
                    (oh you standing always opposite)
I ran barefoot to Madrid

and the skies tell how my eyes
did not meet yours in the street
and I don't know how many pennies
you got from the old wretch
for pawning my coat!

It's all neat again. My coat's on my skin.
Father is on the wall. Opposite.
Madrid is white. And you in my tomb.

THEY BUILD HOUSES IN EIN HAHORESH

They build houses in Ein Hahoresh just like the rest of the world.
First they lay a foundation,
they add walls, and finally
they pour the reinforced concrete roof.
Maybe it's crazy, but I'll try
with my own hands, maybe
in my last years,
to build another house. First I'll pour concrete
the size of my body, without doors.
I'll install a window
(why do they leave the windows for the end?)
and if I don't have a big enough foundation
for my head,
I'll call through the window
to you, my love.

GIVE A SIGN

Give a sign   a sign   a sign
to the shore. To me. Don't call my name,
kiss the ice floating. Pound at the wall
like a prisoner. Like the condemned—his head.
Like one who goes up to the gallows, built
knowingly
by the defendant
with bare hands
with teeth that bit off the iron bars
he loved. Disgusting to think one could
want American ice cream and you
with the same lips
blessed by a penny. With a river's urge
to return to the mountain. To accept
without stretching your neck to the knife
without a sack of tears
on the back. And to say
it is so. To get used
to autumn.
Yesterday.
Today. Again.
Your closed eyes! I am two steps from you.
Maybe we weren't meant for anything
worthwhile. Of negotiable
value. Maybe we'll only be formed out of scorched
earth. So what. I refuse to die
in amity.
In bird-down.
In a life of nothing.

LORD OF HOSTS

1

Bulls did not come to the arena to fight
but to mourn. And their eyes, they tell us,
the bulls' eyes are color-blind!
If only that silly rag would touch them,
like lightning, a call of salvation,
their blindness would split the darkness
of arenas and cities. And like fire
in a thick forest, their dumbness would burn
in a final light smashing
the blood   my blood

is silent. Flocks of cooing flags
on my roofs. And not one rag.
One rag,
Lord! In exchange for my eyes.

2

Maybe—this too is courage. Maybe
glory in a drained cup of wine.
But this is terrible. So terrible
to wake up at morning without a dream
to a day.
To a day.
A day spread precise as the sleeves
of a white shirt on a clothesline.

3

Your landscape in light. In full light
my hands. In a glass aquarium
a gold fish stares
at me. (Daughter. Daughter. Where did you buy
the gold ribbon on your head?)
I will come, my daughter,
to turn on the light in your window.

THE CHOIR STARTED SINGING

The choir started singing. And I hated the chorus
without knowing why. I sat in the first-row balcony,
my eyes backstage.
On stage the ghost was still speaking,
and I looked for the leading lady
who wasn't afraid to cut her veins
now backstage eating
a pear
or an apple
or trying her luck with her garter.
On stage the ghost was speaking.
I looked for the king
who washed off his sins with a jump in the water.
How will they revive him
backstage?
With mouth-to-mouth resuscitation or with a solemn promise
of wages? If he dies properly
in three months.

My prima ballerina! How superbly you were stuck
like a spear in a chocolate cake. And a whole world
moved around you,
revolving on an axle.
Do you, do you also
still flutter backstage
like a toy,
do your eyes in false eyelashes cry
the words of the song?
The choir stopped singing. They came out and bowed.
They have come out and bowed
and gone.
A backdrop.
On stage a blood-colored
pool.

MY LITTLE SISTER

(*Aḥoti Ktana*)

1968

To Michael and Shlomit

הֵם בָּאוּ עַד חוֹמָה.
בַּלַּיְלָה הַשְּׁבִיעִי עַד שַׁחַר אוֹר
שָׁמְעוּ מִן הַחוֹמָה אֶת הַטּוֹבְעִים בַּשֶּׁלֶג
מִבְּלִי רְאוֹת אֶת פְּנֵי הַצּוֹעֲדִים
בְּרוּחַ הַלְּבָנָה:

They came as far as a wall.
On the seventh night into the dawn
heard from the wall the drowning in the snow
not seeing the marchers' faces
in the white wind.

Part One

1

Came as far as a wall. The iron ring
of the chime caught in a mass
of ice. They seized it, rubbed it
like holding the face of a frozen man,
Until the morning light
with invocations, with weeping nails;
begged the voice of the bell
to tear from the frost,
from the killing silence.
And the iron did not shake.
Nor tremble.

2

But we took with us the craziness
of a dog gnawing the moon in a puddle.
And it rang. One
awful ring. How is it
animals and birds inside the wall
did not freeze at this voice!
Nine sainted Sisters
hurried to the gate. Their voices withered.

Naked. Braids on her breast—
my fragile sister!
Standing at the door.

3

My sister's eyes search the wall of the convent
for a scarlet thread. A candle trembles
in the nuns' hands.
Nine holy Sisters look at my sister

seeing—ashes that speak.

4

Dawn that wakes from fears. In light
wrenched from smoke, three chestnut trees
appear this morning
as if emerged from the land of the living:

my sister sees them close by.
My sister does not cry out. Only a catch
of joy in the throat. Nine nuns
are silent in black to my sister
like faces of monuments in a foreign city.

5

The bell rings six.
The Dominican Convent is awake.
The Sisters search my sister's eyes.
My fragile sister!
Nine Sisters look at you
uneasy

seeing—ashes that speak.

6

Angels go with my sister.
A flock of angels goes with my sister
as far as the doorway. My little sister!
She has taken another god,
a gate opens for her.

And a court.

7

Nine "Little Sisters" in a gold frame
shining with inner light.
Doves ate
from their kissed hands,
When my dove came down at the foot of the wall,
torn wing,
their palms were gathered
in supplication,

pink as prayer beads, joints of their fingers
knock now,
while my sister stands at the door.

A n d   t h e   s o n   s e e s
A n d   t h e   f a t h e r   s t a r e s .

8

A cloister's wall is high.
A wall of silence
still higher.
A ladder leans to a wall.
Tops of chestnut trees touch and recoil
from the bell tower.
Three chestnut trees
out of a land of lakes

and mud.

9

From here the world of the living
is seen.
From here a whole world watches
my face dissolve into
blue.

My sister is in the wall.
The waylayer at the gates.
In a heavy night robe,
in bare feet,
spying behind her back
god comes near.

10

The court is amazed. What yearning streams
through my land
—that bitch!

These starving eyes
ripe with love.
Silences
and velvet steps!
Such clean hands and pure minds!

From his suffering image,
from the feet of the cold statue,
look, with a delicate hand
dust is swept
into a gold coffer—
only my crucified memory
outside the fence!

In the court,
in a private language, my sister plays
with another god.

Walls of the house are bright.
No woman has crouched to give birth
on the floor.
No man screams
blood. Their beds
are made ready with pardons.
Small pardons drop
in the lap like a whore's pay.
And his light dripping warm.
If you will not come to us
—how shall we be consoled?

12

Night after night
the Sisters breathe hard in their beds
as if raised on a ladder.
Their bodies shake.
And on this night too, heavy with longing,
the gowns on their skins are burning.

In his high place,
quiet as a tree alone,
he stands.
And light of the mother and the father
trickles down from his face.

Then his bright body breaks out
of a gold frame.
Lord! He comes down
on a ladder of thorns.
His blood is not running.

He swings
in his thin limbs.

13

The granter of grace to the innocent
comes.
He arches over me, saying:
you are my daughter—
The sun.
The frost.
The heat.
All of them pierce my flesh.
His blazing forehead on my face
and the great sea in me.
No world but he.
None but he in me.

Only the soul is awake and knows
that this is the lust of knowing.

14

To give to love the
walkers in the snow. The
pressed. The
oppressor. All the
lost for they are lost.
To bring them back
in pity
in open arms
in ringing bells
in blood.

Nine Sisters drenched with pleasure.
Morning rises
for love.
My little sister
is scared.

15

The world that watched
withdrew.
Her beautiful doll,
father's gift,
they crushed in the snow.

No mother, no brother,
hands crossed over her growing breasts,
they waved my sister
through that gate.

Hid her within the wall.
With sainted patience
the ladies wait.
They are flooded with mercy.

My fragile sister!
No harbor—betrayal
—no island.
Only a folded sail in a storm.

Part Two

16

Far, far
a city lies. Body still warm.
Bells are ringing.

17

You have not seen a city thrust on its back
like a horse in its blood, jerking its hooves
unable to rise.

Bells are ringing.

City.
City.
How mourn a city
whose people are dead and whose dead are alive
in the heart.

Bells.

Now the Sisters are ready.
Ringing,
the bells chime their longing
into fixed rations,
into appointed times
for payment. And the wall keeps them
from the world.
Nine "Little Sisters" pace in awe.
Their robes float. In procession.

My sister sits at the window. She
waits for a brother.

18

i

You never knew Vilk. He takes me
in his paws. He wets my eyes
with his warm tongue,
and when he says good night like this,
I hear my father's sandals
going to his rooms.

Tomorrow Vilk will carry me in his teeth,
and I will be like one of the whelps.

ii

One
bell for prayer.
A second bell
for danger.

A long rope hangs from one.
My sister's life
from the second.

Free of god,
the dog listens for the hidden bell
in the gate of the convent—
day and night.

iii

He never barks.
Before an alarm
he only bares his teeth,
and his eyes are filled with blood.

Then Vilk would set this creature gently
in the secrecy of the kennel. He would cover her face
with his hairy body,
and stand over her trembling. Mute.

When he was murdered, my sister washed Vilk
from head to foot
and wrote: my brother,
in the sand.

19

Christina is lame. She opens her day
with a murmur of eyelashes. Like a dove alarmed from its nest.
Christina circles his face,
a loose wing pleading.
Christina hazards her life
till he will take her to himself.

Christina knows there are endless ways,
but only one
she can choose.
Christina knows fulfillment
is promised,
the gates of heaven in range of her prayer.

A life for our Sister Christina—
but no perfect healing.

20

The second Christina (one God
but not one father) is a red-fleshed
virgin, an excellent mare.
Only the look!
The stricken look when the sun is shining.
And something not conceived
as love.
Heat comes.
Ice comes.
She labors to sleep,
our Sister Christina. All day long
in rage she drives the little Sisters—
all day long
the virgin kneels.

Suzanne is alien. If not to the mother of god,
then to herself.
When there's a tolling to prayer
from the tower,
her head flinches unknowing
as from a whip.

22

No!
Don't imagine
a lovelier one than Marie!
My God—
Oh God, keep
far away
the steps of my prince!

Irena and Olga are glorious with love.
When they sink down
together
to kiss his thin body,
rinse
his mute face with warm
tears,
my sister's frozen eyes
say:
Blessed are the crucified
thus crucified!

24

Our hearts invented a place,
yes, a place in the world
where we would know life without end.
Your lives, how they seize the future!
To our Sister Clarisse—the world
is a waiting room to be prized.

Blessed the Creator! For He has
in His world: such a Sister,
such patience,
such waiting rooms.

25

Most blessed of the nuns the holy flesh
already hallowed by sin.
In the grades of importance,
she is the clapper of the convent.
Not by her loud voice,
but by her great legs
towing the mystery of the world.

She knew it. In her lips—
Scorched straps—it is chained,
shredded as a clothesline.
The holy flesh, our Sister!
With head thrust forward she is the first
who marches to confession
like a battering ram to a wall.
A statue could be shaped
from the stuff in her! And add a drawn sword.

She
pities my sister.
And does not like
black sheep.

Part Three

26

My sister loves the Mother Superior.
A hood covers her clear forehead,
not her shivering heart.

My sister sees the Mother Superior.
Maybe her heart shakes with too much fervor.
Maybe she also has no
place to escape.

When the sun fornicates with the invaders,
the Mother's eyes
store up the spring;

when she faces his high image
in her small
thin shape—the cross drops down.
Body to body
silent. Except for the eyes.
Maybe at the end of time we shall know whom to blame
that now such a heart
is split!

Every day Mother Superior dins hymns
in my sister.
She chants to her and does not speak.

My sister sings in another choir.

27

Oh one who commanded us to be children
quiet
and frightened.

The day I turned back
when a black cat crossed my path!

The day I wept for the neighbor's daughter
when her bridegroom found an empty bucket!

Oh night grinding
sleep! Fear entered all my bones
—I cut my nails at the window!

Every Sunday
my window shakes from the bells of Saint Mary:
every Sunday
my heart is dumb, fearing
the dread of the deep—

Oh one who commanded us to be children
more quiet than fire.

28

My sister sits happy
at her bridegroom's table. She does not cry.
My sister will do no such thing:
what would people say!

My sister sits happy
at her bridegroom's table. Her heart is awake.
The whole world drinks
kosher chicken soup:

the dumplings of unleavened flour
were made by her mother-in-law. The world is amazed
and tastes the mother's confection.

My sister-bride sits. A small dish
of honey beside her. Such a huge crowd!
Father twisted
the braids of the ḥallah.

Our father took his bread, bless God,
forty years from one oven. He never imagined
a whole people could rise in the ovens
and the world, with God's help, go on.

My sister sits at the table in her bridal veil
alone. From the hideout of mourners
the voice of a bridegroom comes near.
We will set the table without you;
the marriage contract will be written in stone.

29

Oh one who asked for the hand of my sister.
Oh one who closed in on her in the valley
to kiss her on the mouth without witness.
With lips tasting clay,
my bridegrooms,
go, look for her now.

We put her at the foot of the wall
that understands silence.
We put her on the mound
like a naked stem.
Blessed be he among men
who will bring her to his rooms,
my bridegrooms!

30

White
white
white
in white

the Dominican Convent prays:
God's estate is draped with quiet flowers,
flooded with profound salvation.
What shall we do for our sister
and she like a wilted tendril?

31

A usual morning.
The light of each separate star still
visible.
A bright point of light like an aimless balloon.
My sister
tries to catch

through the grille!
The light-moth spins off,
the window is frozen.
With a patch of muslin
from the dress of her doll
she stretches her hand for it,
does not despair.

32

To watch with soft eyes
the rising morning. Wipe from the lips
the taste of hot ash.
To bring back
a world to innocence,
as if to its socket a bone
from the foot of the dead.
To return there!
To the city,

and plant there again chestnut trees
in the square,
common bellflowers
near the fence,
and not to fear,
not to fear that the beating darkness
will suddenly close up your sobs
in the bars of a song.

Fragile, my sister!
My fragile sister.

33

In the whisper of chestnuts, in the foaming earth
filled with dark signs,
in the beat of the heart
like a flock of gulls bursting toward you,
in a smell of moss
in the wall,
in joy rising from fissures,
like water collected in cracks,
at the door of your home, my sister,
spring

spring
spring lords over the land!
Already dawn opens wide in the valley.
Only your angels are late.
They give no sign.
They will not say when.

Perhaps a rider will return.
Perhaps the brother.
In the woods my sister plays
hopscotch
with the messiah.

34

A tortured forest. Leaves and crown sacrificed
to a violent autumn.
Bare,
against stars of hostile brilliance,
contrived to guard tubers of spring.

My home carried its roots
to the stake.
With what—
with what, little sister,
shall we weave and draw the dream
now?

Part Four

35

i

In seventy-seven funerals we circled the wall
and the wall stood.
From the promised land I called you,
I looked for you
among heaps of small shoes.
At every approaching holiday.

No man will cure,
nor heaven,
the offense of your scalding silence.

My blessing
did not light your eyes.
My curse
came too late.

ii

—to say good-bye to you
even in one word
whispered

that you were no burden to us.
On the way.
Mother walked heavy.
I.
All your brothers.
And the desperate convoy.
Our strength did not give out,
only the earth below gave out.

iii

No entry to sheds.
On cold stoves.
When we made our beds on steaming
dung.
Before eyes wet
with rotten joy.
In the face of dogs
too proud to bark—

even when shame came into all my limbs,
with transparent nails glaring,
we clung to our flesh
as if alive.

Until we lay down our heads
one near the other.
Until we saw our faces
one within the other.
At the edge of the redeeming pit,
my sister,
we remembered your going alone.

36

You were not privileged to be condemned to death.
You did not enter a convenant of blood.
On the day when you will be spoken for—
behold you
are consecrated
more than eagles
and angels.

37

I vow by you today.
We will not speak, for better or for worse,
of a world that went to ruin. Oh terror—
how will this passage of our lives
be told now.

38

This night, only snow.
Put your face
in the path of the dogs.
Put on the dress
our mother sewed for you,
the only one
left, in white folds.

We have no other dress.
We have no other prayer.
This sun,
no other.
Let us rise up, oh sister,
your time has come!

39

Behold you—behold
they.
So long as the night covers you like a canopy
let us go forth.
Say to them nicely
thank you.
Be grateful
for every hour
of refuge.
Perhaps they were not guilty—
there is always someone more guilty:
(the victim)
(the victim)
Perhaps they heard
only the voice of their hearts:

Go, they said.
Go.
My fragile sister!
You must
go.
Come, sister,
quiet.
Quiet.

40

We knew what the hazards were—
to cross the soft earth,
to pass by the glowing iron
and to say to a stranger
—a world was here.

It comes upon me from behind
—a choir of stones
here!
In the unrepenting street of the city
the shorn head of my sister
breaks out of a wall.

41

sealed in a tomb
unhealed   troops of scorpions rake me
steal me out, take me   voice of my love
(door)
(door)
house of clay   house of life
undo me   renew me
(door)
(door)
my love like a deer
who finds me who floods me   who fills me
delight when I   sorrow
my love who speaks   near now
(over)
(it's over)

Part Five

42

As the fire died. Still everyone stays,
and already everything
has gone out—the flames,
the vault of heaven,
the clothes,
and the brightness
in the eyes of those who stand off.

The noble will rush together then
to those who were burning. To throw water
on every man
—is there a stone boiling still in their hearts?

43

As in a flood dammed too late,
they will come, come to the shore,
their hearts full of pity, to set
the survivors with swollen feet
in the book of chronicles,

to extend a brother's hand!
And they gave them a hand
in spite of their ugly smell.
And before heart and reason could separate
they cried,
and applauded them.
As in a melodrama that ended:
the *characters*
are asked
to step before the curtain!

44

They came out.
They stretched their whole hands to the bread
still fearing hunger.
They stood.
When they smelled plates of soup,
they unwrapped tin spoons
from their leggings.
And all who came near, when they gnawed the bones,
seemed oppressors or thieves.

And they rose up.
In Europe the sun was shining,
and they
bought black umbrellas
as if they were daggers;

and while you stood trembling
I wanted to say to you,
my sister!
Tomorrow they will be first to forget:
they will cover up my blood.

45

The Bikur Ḥolim Hospital
walls soaked
with the smell of sour urine
and dying hopes.

In the old hospital
among walls of red brick
my sister died.

She was two hours old. Suddenly
her eyelids contracted to look—
my sister did not scream.
She was not introduced to the world.

46

You are silent
But our mother used to light
a candle for the saving of her soul
every day.

The candles ran out in the ghetto, and the oxygen
in the shed:
my mother kindled her soul
on all the seas.

Our mother mourned a daughter
who never came into the world.
Eight years. The rest of her sons were cut down,
and she lamented them,
and she mourned my little sister
who never came into the world.

                          —You who saw
everything.
You who saw us,
mother!
How mourn to our faces
someone
who never came into the world?

And the mother stared at me for a while.
And she stared at me for a long while.
Until her lips parted to speak,
and she said, my son
—she was not privileged to see
the light of the day!

And she came close.
And she prepared the candle.
And her hand was holding
another wick.

no one will carry my mother's bier with me
no one will come close to my mother's bier with me
come to the vast plains
lead your eyes to the white river
it scoops out its channel and shoves
like the prow of a heavy
ship in the ice
and say with me
imi
imi

A PARTING FROM THE SOUTH

(Prida Mehadarom)

1949

To the Givati men

.א

וָקָם אֶחָד בַּשָּׂדֶה
וְקוֹלוֹ כְּמוֹ הַלַּיְלָה הַזֶּה:
״הֲנִגִּיעַ — וְאֵיךְ ?״
זֹאת יֵדַע בַּלַּיְלָה הַזֶּה
— כִּבְכָל הַלֵּילוֹת —
אֲשֶׁר יָקוּם וְיֵלֵךְ.

NIGHT MARCH

1

And someone stood up in the field,
and his voice was like this night:
"Will we get there—and how?"
Who will know? This night
—as on all other nights—
it's the one who will stand up and go.

2 Opening

Suddenly. Old wells gather in the eyes.
All the rivers of my blood—awake in double streams.
The heart is locked. No way to leave. To come in. To get near.
Only the surge of mighty waters and an ancient voice:

Don't move, my friend. Our feet are strange feet here.
My friend moves. And our feet do not belong.
Our footsteps are gone. You are not
the great wanderer here, my friend—
And he stretched out the hollows of his hands, bent down, a
      touching of palms.
And the earth came to him.

Herd after herd, it coos round your feet
with a plundering light. And his feet trace-and-do-not-trace-
"My friend, we shall fall." Then, all of it will come
in a wave to your arms—
this earth.

3   Smooth Stone

A parchment thrown—spread open. Wings of wild birds between
   crags, and the crags close.
No road from here. Only the sinews of paths twist like the seams
   of a scroll.
Torn and scattered—a sea of fallen helmets—hilltops
and Guernica on every hill.

"Guernica on every hill!" we listened to David.
David did not get up.
A shadow walks on smooth stone. A stream, like an ancient echo,
whirls, whirls . . . . and the foot of Azekah is empty.
They stood.
They smiled.
—Maybe they said: Great God of the poor!—
And they made a mound of all the smooth stones.
And they walked, the young ones.

They walked.
Heard spring like first clouds of rain,
not knowing. The canyons opened full.
They listened to their own steps on scrolls of gravel.
The night stunned with blossoms. And dawn:
—how did the streams rise in the wadis?
A red tide, as far as Grar.

Torn goat-flesh, offerings of Kedar, floating on the water.
Red stones too heavy to sink.
Breathing stones returned to the surface of the river.

4   A Desert Wind

I loved my heart. Here it is, spread on the sand.
Fingers stammer in the dark: gravel or body?
The sand of trenches shakes in my mouth.
If the cycle of light is endless,
why should faces stay in silence now
on the bewitched skyline?

Face after face in a thousand cradles.
Infants of my life go up to bind a hump of mountain—
The south wind rises. Sand moves in ropes.
The cradles rock:
a thousand babbling of Now.

The trigger is locked until the hidden voice
calls.
No.
Not for weeping.
Only until—
"One more minute of silence."
They get up.
The belt.
The bayonet.
And a crumb of sand
in my mouth.

MIRAGE OF SAND: SOUNDS FROM NEARBY

I bought my son a little bell.
My son, who won't use his right hand,
took the little bell in his hand
and rang with his left.

There are bells all over the world.
Frogs croak, but not for prey.
When my son rings the little bell,
Tamar and Amnon sigh.

And at night I see a strange forest—
Beautiful, the bewildered eyes of the ram!
And a bell on the neck rings, rings.
And barbed wire runs after him.

And all the walls are thick. The houses mute as books.
Maybe the blue sea hears
how ashes sprout in the desert.

Don't cry for the proud ram, my son.
Ring the little bell with your *right* hand—
I'm with you, until night comes.

A BATTLE

Suddenly. Old wells gather in the eyes.
All the rivers of my blood—awake in double streams.
The heart is locked. No way to leave. To come in. To get near.
Only the surge of mighty waters and an ancient voice:
—"We're getting close, closer. You're not the only one,
you, moving there between the bullets!"—
I'll keep the star, too small to hand down.
And the memory of a big hand on the oars—

My friend, did you, too, hear on the way:
"You, you'll come back from the midst of the bullets!"
Was it your star too, the one in the void,
before your heart was spread on the parchment stone?

RADIO SILENCE

Wind in the garden. Wind in the ashes.
How many years did Dambam see flowers?
Hidden like light in a book.

Trenches. Shlomit stood in the sand.
—Why did you put up this roadblock?
No one should come before I get to you!
You didn't cry my name,
you said "Mother"
and I came,
because I'm the one who is coming to you, Dambam.

I am the one to make gardens grow
on the roads you mined at night.
I am the one who will hold your big face,
who will ask for pardon and will spread my good shirt
when the barbed wire burns—blind.

My blood is still. Seeing you return
this way—wrapped by the braids in my lap,
and only my skin then like foolish ripples
—I saw a cloud
gone—
where does the cloud go now, my God.

The silk of the gardens shimmered. He touched mirrors—ashes.
His eyes gnawed the fallen leaves. Clods of earth turned wild:
     barbed wire!
The wind went south. And leafed through the paths like a book.
The night—old.

He moved. He crawled. The barbed wire split at his eyes.
A cyclamen stuck to his cheek—"Where
does the last path twist? The shining path."
And for the first time in his life Dambam saw flowers
torn in his nostrils.

MIRAGE OF SAND: GATES OF THE CITY

Who set fire to the city
and did not wake the city?
Its fields rise like parchment
scorched for three nights.

I will not know the city
if a dog did not wake the city.
It burns like sunset
for three long nights.

A wind comes from the sea. White as plunder
on the charred ruins, clouds in the birds' flight.
The sky is low. On a lane climbing up
to the pyre, a scared man walks in the night.

The shepherd faces the city,
stands at an unhinged gate.
And the city is still as an empty well,
only a red dog waits.

The shepherd keeps wiping his eyes.
His herds low to the flames.
And the city answers like torn flesh.
And the shepherd does not know its name.

A LEAVE TILL MIDNIGHT

Each part of you.
And grief in your body. And the song pours full
in your hands. Because it came,
because silence came.

My hand touched everything I knew in you.
A body blends with me, slips away and returns,
always returns in its curves. Waves.

Now all of you is with me. Since it's good for me this way. Look:
sand waves are still in my hand. For ninety nights sands of fear
ate at the butt of the moment. The spark of our eyes. For my
    coming.

Understand, girl, why a wild man rose from the heat
of your body now
—and no stranger—
and cried without
stopping.

My girl. The next ones go, here they go
after me.
In the confused furrow
the ploughmen will cover my blood.

MIRAGE OF SAND: NIGHT OF THE SIEGE

All the entries are clear,
clear for the shepherds' lambs
and open for those who look up as they march.

The iron gates could not hold—they groaned at the hinges,
collapsed at the foot of the one
hole.
A thin cry.
Like stretched-out giants. And the moon grazed in the hole.

And the night is large and ancient. The guards of the gates
strut at their posts,
dog tags on their necks
—who threaded them with silver chains?

The guards pause and hear
the echo of their steps in seven gates.
The echo rises in the crags,
sprays from their sides—

A crowd of children
goes up from the city
to the top of the pool
to fling green dog tags in the air.

The guards are attentive. Sobbing after them
like a thirsty herd: their footprints,
the locked-up tree and a last dog sniffing a storm in the wall.

The guards shiver: a wind comes. Smell of harvest.
In the passage mined
on the path to the crag,
a starling stands
and sings:

White houses have grown
as far as that gate
down from all the crags.
On the doorpost,
father nails a shining dog tag.

Then blind with fear, he ripped the dream
—the first of the seven guards—
and saw—and saw as far as terror.
His brothers are mad. They talk with the deep.
And stand.

VOICES FROM THE HILL

This is Ḥirbet Fatatah!
Who set the fire in Kharatiya and Ḥata?
A fire was set in Kharatiya and Ḥata.
The rising fire—is it from Kharatiya and Ḥata?
Fire rises from Kharatiya and Ḥata.
Is there anyone still in Kharatiya and Ḥata?
No soldier nor man in Kharatiya and Ḥata.
This is the commander.
And who ordered the fire in Kharatiya and Ḥata?
Those who set the fire in Kharatiya and Ḥata.
The enemy—in front of us.
And who walks behind
and chars our footsteps to Kharatiya and Ḥata?
The deserted clay huts are burning. And the fire opens wide
and the fire is wild.

The enemy walks in Kharatiya and Ḥata.

BATTLE ORDER

"This is the city. And this is the fence. And the hour will be 005."
They waited like animals. They understood like infants: before
them, a chariot of fire.

Oh green city. Oh trees of the cold avenue.
In the shrubs, like animals, the children of love sniff after you.

Your sleep will be split. One part will wake. One part will die.
They will cross you like beasts.
Children of love. Children of iron. The night is lit from the East.

The trees move back. The hearts move forward. The earth is bare
and raw.
They shiver like infants. They stiffen like animals: 005—a minute
to go.

And someone stood up in the field, and his voice was like this
night: "Will we get there—and how?"
Who will know? This night—as on all other nights—it's the one
who will stand up and go.

DAMBAM'S DEATH

1

Don't touch.
This can't be touched!
It is my ugliness.
And don't cry. A cry can't be red if you don't know
what a body is like on the road at night.

We carried our beauty in our arms—
don't turn back, my girl.
You are at a great frontier.—Kneel once
—and go.

Go, Shlomit. Go and forget.
Candles burn in your tears. Terrible crying. A candle of beginning.
If you will run with light feet at twilight,
arms linked,
don't be afraid my girl, to take
the blessing of a white stone.

And quiet.
A last quiet.
Like snow there on the fir tree.

*

A great silence hears me. And perhaps it is I
who comes for the first time to graze alone on the plain—
Here is the passage. Here is a border mark. And this is my voice
come back from the silence.

2

And they see far away. As a drowning man grips his past in his
    hand
in the flash of one phrase. Cut off.
His eyes absorb the dying memory
of a violet nipple pulled from a suckling
—Mother.
       Mother.
             Put me back, nurse!
No use for the son to trust both of his legs!
He walked.
Wherever he went—everything was
opposite. Grown—he did not return
to suck you, painfully.

He wanted to send you one last word
and there's no such word, mother.
His lips carried many—
the dark,
since it can't be sliced in half like bread,
stays mute, and mine.

The body still quivers like parchment. The stone fades.
Thrown.
        Gone.
From everything already vanished—there is
your grief.
Over my hands.
And my hands hang on your breast. A blood amulet.

And you will stay at the frontier.
In a crystal of roads and river. In a fast of clear words,
so clear there is nothing in them, except the murmur
of a blue warmth on your bed.

Maybe you'll see a sign lit up
in the ashes.
Touch—
Then, all of it will come in a wave to your arms—
this earth.

A ROAD OF CYPRESS ON THE WAY NORTH

1

Slowly, boys. They march behind us. They go north—
What a blind day! They hold our paths in their hands.

A step falls in each step. Is anyone up ahead?
A shadow clutches its shadow. My heroes are silent.

My shadows, shadows. No use to walk behind us!
My heroes don't remember the years of our lives.

2

A step ends in each step. There—the city?
Silence. And nothing but silence. Only young grass—

A big tent moves in the wind. A cypress touches a cloud.
Sunset. A red shadow rises like an echo in its vault.

Oh, my friends, why are you silent? If the silence is not.

A CANOPY IN THE DESERT

(Ḥupa Bamidbar)

1970

To Vitka

קְרַב, סוּסִי. אָנוּ מַפְלִיגִים הַלַּיְלָה שׁוּב. וְלֹא נָשׁוּב
רֵיקָם. נֵצֵא בְּאֵין רוֹאֶה אוּלַי נִתְנַהֵל בְּאֵין מַפְרִיעַ.
אֲנִי חַיָּב לִרְשֹׁם אֶת הַדְּבָרִים בִּשְׂפָתוֹ כָּל עוֹד שְׂפָתוֹ
יֵשׁ לָהּ פֶּה שׁוֹמֵעַ. עַל כֵּן עָלֵינוּ לְדַיֵּק. עַד יִדְלַק
בַּחַלּוֹנָה הָאוֹר נַעֲבֹר
גָּדֵר שְׁנִיָּה, בַּשֶּׁטַח הַיָּרֹק נָרִים וִילוֹן
כָּבֵד. יְשִׁישִׁי עָיֵף. וְהוּא מֵרָצוֹן צוֹעֵד,
אֲנִי מֻכְרָח.

שְׁתֵה, סוּס,
יִהְיֶה מַסָּע צוֹרֵב. כְּאֶל אַלְפֵי אַלְפֵי יָמִים.
אוּלַי לֹא שָׁוְא הַטֹּרַח.

Prologue:
A Green Entrance

Come here, my horse. Tonight we are traveling again. And we will
   not come back
empty-handed. We'll go out unseen perhaps move undisturbed.
I should set the words down in his language as long as his language
can be heard. Therefore we must be precise. When the light
in her window goes on, we'll cross
a second fence, we'll raise a heavy curtain on the green
field. My old nag is tired. But he steps willingly.
I have to.

Drink, horse,
it will be a scorching journey. Toward thousands and thousands
   of days.
It may be worth the trouble.

First Gate:
The Return to the South

AT A CROSSROADS: A SETTLEMENT

1

I laughed laughed laughed,
this joke—a city!
You can cross the district
of your desires on foot. Almost without understanding
I find myself winding
3 times round your capital

the main street. These houses
like bundles of hay tied up afraid
of the first rain. And window frames! Last year's
New Year's cards. A development town
open to dry streams
surrounded by twelve clever commentaries
like the five scrolls—

on benches baked by the afternoon sun
men like old palms
snore to the rhythm of jazz
in a park

not a tree

strange. Men women and even the children wear
black hats, new
with odd peaks,
go out on the street
to stroll

with striped shirts

and the day's wind moves around white and I pass between them
and return
laughing
and cried recalling their childhood

NO ROAD: A CITY

2

So this was a city. The gate—arches. The water
troughs of Avdat flow like the calligraphy
of a precocious child. Now
the palace is already asleep. The Sabbath drunk
pisses in the ditch. The Street of the Potters
loses its smell in the strong perfume
of elegant ladies. The young girls buzz
in the windows. Old-timers walk back and forth
in the street, in the shadow of torches.
I delight in my old women
expert in love.

I ENTERED AVDAT ON FOOT

3

I entered Avdat on foot through the Gate of Spices.
When sunset washes the neck of Mount Eldad
even the faces of women haggling in the market
are flushed with pleasure—
then wink at them! A man who gets
a warm slap from a lovely creature is happier
than a virtuous one as good as dead in a beautiful city.

4

A woman speaks to the priest
and the priest rises dripping from the Spring of Myrrh:
You'd better believe it, Priest, we have no No
fruit that rots, no women that go to waste—
That's so! The sun stands strong
in Avdat. And the wind—let it take you!
—and her laughter goes as far as Bsor.

I might have lived in this street across from the oil press.
Here you can watch how morning rises
from a desert night. Cadets getting ready,
tassels on the general's helmet. And his wife's thighs
touching the heart like a popular song.

I might have lived in these small rooms
that knew how to keep in the cold. I might have fought
the wars of the city

they were no use

ENTRANCE TO GRAR

5

A train stood in the station. The last time. Half of it
lighted. The uncovered head in the window. A woman
I somehow imagined. Like those condemned to disgrace by the
  underground
I saw in a film. Mourners returned to their homes. One wore
a soft hat with a rolled brim. They saw us clearly
and ignored us. A Bedouin child with eyes as big as her face
stretched out her hands
with violets.
Two. For a quarter. Ruined dovecot. Doves do not choose their
  deaths.
Trampled fence. Someone went through, instead of around.
There was a public prayer. Lost speculators
in a coffeehouse forced open. Just for now. The sea
withdraws.

6

My horse's neck bends to the wind he hears
and trembles. If I could speak with eyes open
as he does
I am afraid

someone hums a tune.
The earth continues

Second Gate:
Three Days Abstaining from
Speech

LIMESTONE AND SAND

7

Come.
We came into sand. The moon still hangs above us. When it too
    spills away
the world around us will be whole and withheld. Already
there is no way back. Paved
roads are behind us. Far behind, a fictitious world
stays. We won't know
what's ahead. Except that it's hushed
now and no one between us
no witness. You are around me

and within me
it flows

AND BELOW US IT FLOWS. SLOWLY.

8

Forget that anything else exists. Now in the white plain
it twists
around the birds' swaying hill. Tomorrow
it will sweep the hill away
wild in its rocks it spreads its folds and stretches
in a frozen slope, wanders,
closes a circle, returns and makes
a bank
a new wave

like the pages of a long debate

continuing

I CAN LEAF THROUGH THEM

A long terrible
debate

and the blue is a canopy

RED

9

And the red
is bloodred. Skies fenced in a swarm of granite. Long fingers. Eyes
of the high court see. 600,000 statues breathe in the cliff. My face
is chiseled in profile. Before
I began my image was carved
in the bedrock. There must be
a way to get out
to break through! To make a shortcut. To be a fault
a red tunnel
and the sand comes near. I am full of it
it turns in me

the pages of a debate
continuing

THE TIME AND THE PLACE

10

To find the lawn I watered yesterday.
To find the house with the slanting roof.
To find the door with the paint peeling.
To come inside and tell you, woman!
What do you know if you were privileged not to know
a taste of return.

AND A VOICE ENGRAVED

11

Don't make fun of me, my love. I won't go
nor will I let you stand splendid
and aloof, behaving like a spoiled child. I can still afford
a clean dress
but not another hope

AND DON'T CHOOSE

12

Don't choose sterile words for me.
In Hebrew more deadly than yours I could write down
a smooth list of charges against me
and improvise here

with my own hand. On a typewriter. Even
with copies. Or with a burnt-out match
for engraving now in the sand
that flows under me here
indifferent as an EKG

COME

13

Get rid of the mask of blank
seriousness. Don't face me like a judge
with his eyes gouged out who admits every despised piece of paper
as evidence

and not my breast. My labored breathing. Not a screaming poem
I never could write
"In the crest of the waves against
the fangs of the rock." I am tired. I made chalices
from my hands

TWO PERFECT CHALICES

14

Transparent glass. My hands. I filled them
with warm sand. Urgently. I closed my eyes
in a desperate bet
I swore them in as a blood amulet
(let one grain not drop from my hand
let one   not drop)
when I grew weak and the joints of my fingers turned white
with strain and the sand slowly spilled from them
at first
grain by grain and then
all at once
like my confidence quitting—I knew

THAT ALREADY

15

It's decided.
Would come. Would come back. You would come
in order to go without coming back.
We won't even be given the time
to correct what we did not do
by mistake

A VOICE OVERCOME BY ECHOES

16

. . . . and maybe
I didn't want to return. For a minute—
like a dream to shift the curtain
with a swing of the hand and from the hideout
just blow on your face
a speck of surprise!

I don't know why
there are so many haunted words for this
in the dictionary. After all
I came into the sand.
And I keep on moving
an hourglass
from sand
to sand

UP TO A HANGING MOON

17

At the white pump handle
on the plateau spilled out
dawn after dawn I look for a space
with no barrier, return and climb
to another place to bleat to you in Morse code:

I

w
a
n
t
e
d

t
o

c
h
o
o
s
e

Third Gate:
First Encampment
and Meeting

18

This is the red canyon. This is my open city.
If you did not come for the harvest
please be welcome under the shadow
of my sand. Oh young man,
please forgive an absentminded one who sobered up
from his wine, and nothing quite right
with the day.

Swallow your pride, rider. In the desert
I've learned to call my glass—mother
and the most lowly lizard
—sir.

Because a lizard looks for a master.
The rope claims a tower.
The bell rings
so the shamed will lift up their heads
to praise heaven.

THIS TOO I LEARNED IN THE DESERT

A man needs a lizard.
A shadow claims a solid
body, otherwise it shakes
and the shadow might be untamed
with no first body to lean against
an iron-edged stick
for marching safely on

the sea of tears

it soaks in very
fast

you know. The law of the sand
flows. Stronger than
anything else.

19

They came this far and here
they did not make themselves known. Footsteps in the canyon
simply left no trace.

You are silent. Praise the unknown mutes!
Whose importance we don't realize
only feel their existence
perhaps on this side of heaven. Is that your horse?
Mine.
And does he move too?
You can see for yourself.
Marvelous! What is he made of?
Water.
Shit! What can you do with water?
A horse. A desert.
And who made him so beautiful?
My mother.
You ingrate! And you left your mother there—

(FAR FAR A CITY LIES)

Her daughter-in-law kindles the fire for her.
Blessed are those who love! Take
this, my gift for the journey. Free
for the sake of friendship. Just a flower
of sand. Not afraid of the sun
it won't fade—
I can bet your horse on it
they're alike. Already our body collapses
and forever it

stays

LOOK: SPEAK! SPEAK!

20

Fiber of pure granite
waved from one hand: statues of the decisive
First Day. A granite column rises
kneels before its creator—
we
and they
—aren't we the most primeval of god's creatures
and too weak to wipe out
our arrogant stubbornness!

COME WITH ME TO THE CREEK OF INSCRIPTIONS

21

A shark rolls in the creek of Inscriptions
gaping in dry dust
the wadi passage under fire and sometimes
a wind comes and it is a scalding grace
and a blind mailman in a red hat
turns round
on the rocks
an ancient creek, creek of Inscriptions
tattooed letters bloom
in the stone's cheek
and a rose carved
in the lattice
and a well-defined donkey
and a hot name and a slanting arrow and an open
heart
petrified together

TO LIVE WITH CHRONICLES

22

To live with sun this brass
this polished mirror. With drifting
sand boiling
in the lungs
the liver. To carry rock
after rock
to shift all these letters
to the dead
sea

and to move step by step like a scar
on the backs of railroad ties
and not to search
not to search for cities

of refuge

IF I HAVE FOUND FAVOR

23

Those who say *amen* don't see
those who say *amen* don't hear
those who say *amen* only those
get up in the morning free:

the sand sheets are disordered.
A hasty *amen.*
An abandoned bottle.

24

As one who goes to a remote place.
In swollen
shoes. In a black coat. His shirt collar
buttoned
with a stranger's eyelids squinting against
the washed blue of the sky
plateau beat down
see, I said to myself, here too,
a monk. Perhaps the divine is hidden
in a place where no one waits.

FORGIVE ME, HOLY FATHER

25

You did not meet a saint, boy,
nor monk. It's a man who comes.

From a city?

Whose sirens were stilled.

And your business here?

Selling balloons.

In the desert?

In the fault, my boy.

IMPOSSIBLE TO COMMUNICATE

26

You fell on your head, man! Or you really
see—

Selling balloons
for no reason.

Smuggler. Where to?

My son. You've just fancied me a saint
and already I seem like a thief!

It's all the same! Of course you escaped
here—from where?

—Stop!
May thunder strike me. May I drop dead
on the spot if I tell you a lie!
Fear of the sacrosanct is greater
than fear of a sword.

A THOUSAND YEARS

27

            I built on sand.
A thousand years like one day.
I built a thousand years less
one till one day
all was lost
              a thousand light years
from now on I will dig with fingers
down to the flesh the blood
until I hear their voice a voice
tearing the desert   coming back
split in long burrows
in the dry waste

that was not destroyed. That won't be destroyed
again.

IN AN INSTANT
MORE SUNS ARE KINDLED

28

Their light hovers. A white-hot shovel rules the fire
Scorches our footprints
(no one will come through!
no one will come through!)

The bays are wide open. And our sea
is finished and gone.

FROM ANOTHER HOMELAND

29

And a frozen shriek
like an ice stroke suddenly a spread of wings
pours shadow
falls on sand and pure stone
—a buzzard
a raven from another homeland
someone celebrating at a high altitude.
Close
as a light returned from a lonely island
a single tooth flickers—
maybe the man carved his mother's name
in the sand with a gold tooth
before he collapsed

TWO FOR A QUARTER!

30

Balloons
　　　　colorful
　　　　　　balloons!
We were strangers in the town's celebrations
we are here.
　　　　　Round
　　　　　　　and around
not in circus gates. Not in the neighborhood
market. Far from the renovated
walls my balloons glow
like street lamps
—quarter
　　　　quarter
　　　　　　　two for a quarter!
　　　　　　　　　　　Fresh
　　　　booty
in a blaze

THE COLORS OF THE RAINBOW

31

From a blue sleep:
From a gold blossom:
From a blushing girl:
and thin as heaven
transparent as a bride's face
greener than young lawn
childhood returning
from the land of Ofir
their skin a string / snaps like tidings /
the blue of their eyes / over a vast land /

go round, my stick! Wave
a crown of colors. Blooming forever.
From all my pure
infants.

32

I heard that you know how to plant a tree
and make a whole celebration for it
with a little soil and many words.
Watch! Honest people from the north, come
and watch!

I planted young balloons in the sand
they grew

balloons
without water. Without intricate
tools without ceremony
only a salt wind. With sky

LOTS OF SKY

33

And sit near. All day close
hand in hand
without dangerous words to see
only to see how the light fills it
(up)
(up)
(up)
and the sun nests in it
jealous
and when it explodes
it's a tree

planted by streams of sky

Fifth Gate:
A Second Meeting with the Balloon Man

34

You cradled in the wind!
Buy a balloon from an old man
sick of a strange love

TO PLANT IN SHIFTING SAND

35

And not ask
how. Will it blossom
will it bud? When

will groundwater touch the blood
of the single balloon
full of tears

—buy! Since the day has come the day
has come! And they are transparent. They are light
and not yet ripe

—for a quarter! Very first flowers from the King's garden
two for a quarter
buy balloons for planting
the Arbor Day of Sand!

The child is dead.
I am going to him
and he will not come back to me again.

I HEAR WINGS
FLAPPING ON THE SAND

36

Wings flapping. Endlessly.
The world's a glass door. I see. Picking berries.
Dido lifts his legs over the barbed wire. In his hands
a dark berry. Like the blood of the ram. Dido lowers his legs
from a roof beam. Backward. Dido's crooked legs explore
blind
the wooden ladder. Broken. Its rungs—milk teeth missing in the
    center—
it leans against a huge dovecot painted green. Pigeons in the yard
are greenish almost black on their necks and bellies. They must be
thirsty. He says.
At noon Dido eats in less than a minute. Right away wanders
between the tables. He drags a tin pan banging with his left hand
upsetting time in the dining room. Big Calypso has to
eat well. He smiles.

Calypso's a small soft puppy a kind of damp velvet
pillow and one of us. Calypso will grow up
fast. He'll be the finest dog in the place. Dido says. And Dido
will be a vet. Maybe. A watchman in the fields. One of these
days.

Meanwhile the teachers complain. His feet are muddy. His hair
uncombed. How can you be such a mess
son!

YOU HEAR

Dido writes in secret. Once I saw a notebook. Strange. Poems
stuck together from newspaper clippings. Resembling nothing.
A scatterbrained boy. Now he has a watch. The dream of his life
a pilot's watch. Expensive.

Dido comes neat to the afternoon meal
on the Sabbath. White shirt.
Combed. Sweet smelling, hiding a terrible secret. Only a little
shy because soon everyone will say that hateful
thing: what a beautiful boy!

Grew up

you hear? The voice still flaps out there
in the sand. Without stopping.

Sixth Gate:
A Sandstorm Hits a New
Moon's Face

37

We went far. The whites of my eyes blink from rock
to rock like a dream of stone.
How the view opens up at me! The wax earth
continues past the sky. Not to go blind. To keep the pupils
spread wide as windows
to see that in it
only in it
something is created in its image and likeness.

A storm plows over Jebel Libni. In the Valley of Nakhl
a wall of white
sand

MAP OF A STORM

38

Same hem of the sky. Hills
that were shaped are now without
form and name. Something completely mad
a tangled and opaque ball
pours its fury on them

the storm spreads over a huge area.
Will calm down. Will creep after you. Will return again.
Beware! But not too much
it's not a habit of desert sailors
to stop in a ravaging wind. The most veiled woman
has a face that draws
light. Don't be afraid.
Force it to happen. Behind seven veils
there is
there surely is some dune
that isn't a fable. To clutch at.
To fasten down.

39

Like a corpse swinging on a stretcher
silence comes back to the breathing
space. Your horizons always return
from dead storms. They climb from the cleft
in the plain. They root
in bitter water. Only the sand—
unbelievable! Flows
and overflows. It bursts confused and wasted
like semen.

LOOKING FROM ANOTHER ANGLE

40

Her childhood sailed in the seas. My age took
another direction. A dream that comes back clarifies
slowly. We will climb
and will enter the open walls
sand
sand
sand

—maybe we sinned. Dream children! Surely she
surely I
did we really go wrong?

41

Maybe we forgot to count the gates
we carried from town. Maybe we didn't notice
another gate
nailed to the hinge. There was a storm
the storm is darkness. Total. Like an awful light.
The panic's an urge you don't have to learn
bliss of great birds soaring
running of mountain goats to the spring
at evening. Breath of a tiger
circling a spring of live water
at the hunting season.

No. Not all is allowed.
Not all was allowed. And I wanted
to approach like summer. I came
because I came to inherit.

NOW EVERYTHING STANDS STILL

42

The course of the great wadi

I hear something collapse. A tired
mountain. A falling tree.
Maybe a dying enemy.

Seventh Gate:
Letters
Abandoned in the Valley of Nakhl

43

8 in the morning.
My food is wheatgroats. My whole lap—sand.
My eyes full of jasmine.
I write to my loved ones today
tears on my cheeks:

SAME DAY

44

I was an alien to you leaving
not following my heart's command. In front of the house
a crowd of us got up and hurried away.
Now I breathe the dew of their tears
so it is almost more respectable:

45

Is my son still dark and handsome?
I will bring you copper buttons, *waladi.*
You asked for shiny buttons, son.
At the end of the march
I will bring a bright-colored scarf
to the mother who bore you.
　　My father!

I wish I were a fast-flowing river
or even a lightning rod.
To land on the roof of the house
one night

on my couch!

TIME 12:30

46

I gave up my shoes on the white mound.
The coat was left in the canyon.
(I will bring you copper buttons, my son
copper buttons   my orphan)
May Allah pity the well
that tricks me!

See me, my loved ones, in a nightmare
not in a dream.

TIME 21:00

47

I sat on the ground. And the ground was fire.
I rose from the ground. The ground was fire.
I ran
the sea in front of me my face in my hands
and my hands on fire.
There is probably a land
it's part of us—
how the land turns to fire!

MIDNIGHT

48

All the reckoning all the yearning
you've already placed stone over stone. Oh my God!
Discover the eyes of the stars. To help out.
Awful being alone before You.

The wheat field is near
I didn't really go far.

Make me seen and not seeing
the desert rising against me—

my house is beyond the cliff
beyond

49

Your lament is heard since morning.
Sons. Wife. Plunge your face in water
perhaps it will relieve me a little. Only my father
still stays up and waits
at the gate till evening.

He will hop on his crutch. And he will tear and cut
the darkness with his cane
like the sword he used to wave.
  Stop crying! The one I raised in pain
  will come back in the morning. He must.
  I will recognize him by the radiance of his face.

WHY WHY

50

Woman, wash my feet
because the journey was long.
Woman, don't lift your face
until I wash the shame from my face.

A man returns from there
older by one more day.
Returns. Palm trees in his eyes.
Returns. With flags

above him

a day

that was never born

THE EVENING BEFORE

51

My shoes in the Jiddi Pass

THE COAT AT THE OPENING OF THE CANYON

52

To shed like a snake. The skin
from my self. Bite the sun
that dangles its shadow
from its throat! To suck
one cluster
of dew
oh, how much dew
lies on my own
best vine
(a voice tears the desert
a voice tears   )

how the Nile recoiled! Oh God
bring a curse on its sweet
water that did not reach the lips of a man

dying

53

Mountain   all that preceded
the mountain   all that preceded
the mask   that preceded
the word
the barrier   where
did your footprints   disappear?

Proud. My desert is
too proud to answer.

A DIALOGUE AT NIGHT BY ST. CATHERINE'S MONASTERY
A MOUNTAIN BEHIND A MOUNTAIN ABOVE AND RISING
THE MOUNTAIN OF MOUNTAINS

54

A flower is easy to define
not light held from its own speed
on the back of an eroded stone. When the mountain first shines
it releases the down of a bird
from rock:

—Oh. We'll climb to the top!
—I'll wait at the foot.

—Of course we'll go up the mountain!
—I won't go up the mountain.

—And you'll admit you were here and didn't go up?
—I will. Because I stood here.

Soon it will be light. Come on
we'll go up!
—Your head and the mountain! There's nothing
there. Nothing. Except what
cannot be reached
in the light

UNPRONOUNCED VOWELS

55

Blue
the blue of the sky won't be bluer than this

clear
the screen of the mountains of Moab no clearer than this

the horizon is not drawn
with hieroglyphics but with unpronounced vowels. With names

they come
a fleet of names rowing toward you with the long oars

of slave ships

And you go up like someone escaping. Call,
the gate is transparent
and locked. Even if you burst in and tear her veils
she is still hidden from you:

all my shores flooding. And more
than can be expressed in all the vowels.

NO END OR BEGINNING

56

Stone over stone between stones.
The fire.
The drums.
The treason.
When all is silenced when all is dead by His command
and alive
in a light that won't be destroyed
light to light between lights

—will not die!
Will live enslaved. It's not a mistake. No,
no crown for kings
—slavery. Take it! Or
go

LADDER

57

3,000 stairs to St. Catherine's
(they say that it's more)
3,000 days the serfs of the mountain carved
(they say that it's more)
so that St. Catherine's would be laddered in stone
to the mountain of mountains—
As you go down the last thousand
the monastery closes upon you and a voice
from the wall comes back to you
in golden bells:

ALL MY BELLS

The trembling day. The glory of my holy men in black!
The bitter valley lies at our feet
because your dream will never penetrate
the mountain. Forgive them Our Father
forever
for they never understood
the kind of stuff
Jacob's ladder was made of.

58

Honorable judge! Our trial drags on and I lose patience
one has to admit I got mixed up in an unfortunate
ambiguity. Criminal. Almost
like Hebrew grammar like
gutteral letters and the rule
when the throat is full of hard words
that are exceptions to the rule. But how to pronounce it
so it will be clear
with the right intonation in an open vowel
not in a strange accent

(HE SHADES HIS EYES AND ONLY
HIS LIPS MOVE)

59

Not to be caught on thou shalt not sin. Like you,
I was not meant for an indecent act. But I loved
a black girl. You could see the air stir from the mountain!
She bloomed from the sick gray like some kind of unbelievable
    oasis.
I did it to her. In the heat of day. A seething
day
as long as a fast. But now
now on an ordinary day air does not stir from the mountains
and how will I be understood
how will I understand I who committed an act before I heard
a tortured voice.
It was done. Was it really done again?
And this time too I was
trapped! My body sneaks away from itself
and my voice is deafened by the blood pumping
how will I scream let me go let me go
—tyrant! What will I do
you are the desert. And I
make words:

WE WILL GET TO THE BOTTOM OF IT

60

My time my time. Time has really come. I am ready
to quit the game. I will leave you
my beautiful sack with the shells with the branches
of coral with the dazzling fossils with the granite
houses and the salt
provisions and plunder and pruned leaves
all that I haven't collected so far
and mine from my treasure I stole it from no one
what is stone what is chalk
that I should worship it. I already have loosened the sack
here I will unfasten
this all like vows
to testify that I only looked for things
for one purpose
not a purpose maybe neither an end of it
nor a beginning. This time I said I will listen and I will do.
  Like this

ONLY LIKE THIS

61

And afterwards we will say
the essential the whole essential and only the essential
for the truth

BUT IN THE CREEK

62

In the dry riverbed dust upon dust the events
of the journey are written. In two columns. A different column
on each side. One for scripture, two for fear, a story
facing a story. In the most natural place
on the wall of the red canyon one
of my columns
is missing. I don't know how or what
hand plucked my story
in cold blood
(in the thicket
in the thicket)
walls of stone cry at night in a jackal's voice
your story
your only one
you loved

ADMISSION OF GUILT

63

I returned to the festive city to pack my belongings
and I had no time for my few belongings.
I took less than nothing,
then they caught me by the hand. They forbade me
to enter. You're not allowed to enter when the whole city's
out of bounds, celebrating, seeking to be consoled.
You may attack your brother
(shalt murder
shalt murder)
and you won't be pitied if you come among
celebrants in a city that makes desparate efforts
to be happy
while your clothes are blood soaked:

I admit my guilt
but I do not confess.

THEY TOLD ME
BRING ALL THE EVIDENCE YOU HAVE—I BROUGHT IT:

64

I remember the circumstances.
In 1999
A.D. I sit in a summer gathering I take my potatoes
out of the fire. Two new potatoes the way I like potatoes
roasted in the fire. And the one who attacks me from behind
does not have to know
but can see clearly
the potatoes I put in the fire are new
and that I want from the hearth only two potatoes
raked from the fire and already
(there was a tree. And its shadow fell on the ground
   the shadow of a tree)
it was too late to explain
to excuse

SUDDENLY LOOK

65

I remember the facts:

When I threw off my clothes I knew what I was doing.
When I poured sand a handful of sand on my head
I knew why I wanted the sand to spill
to flow over my head to make a sound

when I put the damp shell to my ear
out of an undefined impulse
(a lover's impulse
listening only inside)
I knew that I wanted to suck the coolness
because it's allowed man wants something
like that and there's nothing more beautiful

AN INTERJECTION

66

What would you do, your Honor
if your back's to the sand and only the voice
of the common raven
circles over your head!

Bury it in a red canyon
and it will be silenced.

A SEAT OF JUDGMENT

67

And about the evidence:

Honestly! The charge is full as a marketplace
the clean and the filthy. The side of a temple the side of a pig
the pure and the putrid will save will sin will wish wash fill fall
revolve
in a loose-tongued face. Pairs. An ancient sharp-witted
game. Your Honor! Your Honor!
The burden of proof is not on the man but on the one
who drives him crazy. I asked for mercy.
Maybe this mistake from time everlasting found me
guilty. Because there is no pity in the judgment
of the Law. When law is the Law of men

alive

IN MEMORY OF

68

My expert witnesses
were late as usual
this time too they will stand up tomorrow
in front of the empty ark
of testimony

(forest
forest)
those who stay at the gate.

THE SIN AND THE WONDER

69

They brought me to trial, brother, for perjury.
Could I deny it? There was no one
with me there who spoke
or understood my tongue
cleaving to the roof of my mouth

(if I forget thee Oh canyon!
if I forget thee   )

in a cloud. As in a stone. On all my roads
I imagined I'd find the road

to you

—court was dismissed!

Tenth Gate:
A Canopy in the Desert

70

At daybreak as our enemies were far
their shapes went on reflected in the blue
like an oasis in a mirage
the one who separates the holy from the profane
will not divide us any more, bride!

THE VOICE

71

The source of the voice
is a mountain
phoenix of sand or the dust
of flowers plucked from our fingers

THE VOICE

72

It makes
no difference
the desert
turns over laughing
its lust
is a clanging bell

—I came bride!
—I came bride!

THE HAND OF HER CREATOR

73

In basalt burned out. In indifferent granite
in sandstone still
red from the drop of the covenant
my voice is wrapped in a package of vows
on a land in its time of bleeding:

I will pay for a marriage contract with my best
my chosen from the land.

NUPTIAL AGREEMENT

74

Its cutting light keeps the clay and crumbles
thought to its basic elements. Light
stones life.
His head is uncovered. He is crowned with quiet expectation
the blue of his beloved city hangs in the dust of his eyelashes
the tallow of a memorial candle not used up
sheds fire along his spine
scorched skin at the back of his neck:
I crave this light
for our wedding stage.

THE GUESTS

75

My guests will come from everywhere
we will not know how. Like a smile slight and cunning
their steps fill the white wadi
this is their custom:
first they put out a foot to make sure
and after, they lean their bodies
forward. As if their bodies were glass
beakers and the ground under them
brittle as ice. They have not learned it from cats
or from tigers
they have gathered it from the treacherous land
in evening classes

beloved

THEIR HIDDEN BORDER

76

They heard the voice.
Like flexible antennae my guests
will swarm in the slope

of the plain. Their day was announced in braids of dust
intoned. Their proud solitude in navigation.
In communication they have strange names
statues
birds
sometimes

wild flowers
protected by national park authorities
and plucked one
by one. Come back to meet
name piled on name. But let's not
mistake their identity when communication
is silent. My guests the best of my friends
their instincts do not betray them.
Only once. Hard to grasp

SOMEWHERE

77

And they will not be late. You can
be sure they will be ready to act before
they arrive. Some kind of alarm bell
really exists, a sort of radar
mechanism in the live
space between body and underwear there
next to the sensitive skin it revolves
automatically every day
until like a blink
it turns on. It is still only
a beam
something tiny like
a red light
bent or darting
and that moment
there's no other world
except this flame—

78

Thus the lonely poem. The words are hesitant
go out before the idea. They twist before
fire. With pure bells on the neck
the heralds of the flock slide

to the web of dunes. From this bugged thicket
to winding gorges in a dry cloud
to a ravine our canyon
where the sky is clear as the path of knowledge

—to return to the valley of the lost!
To come together again:

AND YOU WILL KEEP GOING

79

My friends
since they are friends don't need to look at the map
by candlelight. They need only a simple mark
like a stone. And they turn like the color
of a tree forced to bloom in the baldness of sand.
Desert

not desolation not howling wilderness
to them but simply
a desert. And the Name is spelled
in a pocket-size map. Because my friends
and a desert

are many turned one. And one
is the place the one place in the world
where a man will not die alone.

USHERS

80

The day is still long and dreamlike. If you will
there is nothing lovelier. Here
whoever comes comes. And they come running
by the dunes. How do you run in the dunes
that sweep backward and rise in a wave forward
it's hard to understand if you
never ran in pure sand
as I ran through the words of Rabbi Nathan
with burning eyes.

A BRIDEGROOM'S FOOTSTEPS

81

A land touches my temples. A smooth sea rocks
at her door.
My hand on the fringe of the lock
the key sank from my hand
into the well-defined day
I made peace like a shell.
Not raging like clouds. As calm
as a grown-up love story
that winds its light around the neck

of the aging canyon

word
word
word

a bridegroom toward a bride
walks

in the desert:

A CANOPY FADES

82

The glass shattered. The ring closed
and the cry of happiness. Candles burn.
In a shining circle my ushers
embrace a silk canopy

my love is not at my side.

AS A RIVER
AGAINST ITS BANKS

83

I'll flaunt my youth in the gates of Gaza
my love! I'll pursue you. I'll pursue you
because you are stronger than death. Tell it in Gath
tell it! A bridegroom fierce as a mountain stream
defied your sanctuary.
And your father can not hide you.
Your brother will not protect you.
Because I came to mount you I came.
The horns of the altar and oaths
will not save you! Everyone will stand back
on the day you return to fight
your lover.

TO PURSUE

84

A nation great and powerful.
Made of lead letters and tobacco snuff
like one man
they are sitting in the saddles in full array.
In a marching column my friends
wait for the order to move

A second warning. Go out, champion!
Before everything breaks loose. There is a chosen boy
between the two camps. But the sword is still in its sheath.
Your eyes are as beautiful as his. His heart pounds
on your heart in ashes
—desert!

Soul to soul understanding.

ON THE SKYLINE

85

Until daylight's inside me. I won't pursue
I won't pursue any more. Because a chase is finished
but not completed. Like jealousy and balm.

On the sealed skyline
lost blue
look, the impossible is possible:
facing me like an unyielding vow
my love—a pillar of sand.

86

Slowly slowly the pleasure guests will disperse. Will scatter
the words connected together
couch of love's poison. A wandering hammer
crushes burning sand. It's hard for the earth
to be. A bridegroom marches
to be. A bridegroom's heavy footsteps
to be. A bridegroom's footsteps
cross dream lakes

a cup.
A ring. Corals
of tears.
A yellow whale
throws him up on the shore
glistening

behold you
—to a supreme King. Over all the seas.
Alone.

Eleventh Gate:
Last Meeting
with the One Who Plants Balloons
in the Wadi of Paran

87

Look! Like a beggar you still
court your horizons. We meet again
like a combination of names in a web
of white lines. Maybe the time has come
to ask what you are doing here

in a land turning red in stripes

QUESTIONS AND ANSWERS

88

All this time. Were you alone?

Alone with everyone.

I don't want to insist, but an answer
is a working tool like a knife,
man, for bread.

I went to seek.

Asses, or footprints
of sky paths?

I wish I were part of an answer.

You went out to her. So why does sorrow
hang in the grooves of your face?

I leaned on a cane made of
a light beam.

My beautiful prince! Between the imagined and the grasp
the shores of your legend are shining.

At night on my bed my mother used to
sail this boat

89

And tomorrow when your eyes squint
from longing or a blinding light? I will come back.
I think.
And how will you look when you return? Like my father,
I'm afraid, honestly.

Who is your father? I have his name. My mother drew
his portrait in an obscure song:

> *This is Ḥirbet Fatatah!*
> *Who set the fire in Kharatiya and Ḥata?*
> *A fire was set in Kharatiya and Ḥata.*
> *The rising fire—is it from Kharatiya and Ḥata?*
> *Fire rises from Kharatiya and Ḥata.*
> *Is there anyone still in Kharatiya and Ḥata?*
> *No soldier nor man in Kharatiya and Ḥata.*
> *This is the commander.* My name is Dambam,

I was one year old.
So, Dambam my boy, where to?
To be master in your house.

GETTING LATE

90

The man
is silent. Like one split by the blow of an axe he stands in two
till his lips came together to join
words never separated

go

forth

the desert is yours and the world inside the desert and the desert
inside the world . . . and his murmur blurs.
As sand wilts the edge of a blue balloon
through its thin skin the sea appears
as a violet sea, and he is gone.

AND NOW
LIKE ONE EXPECTED AT A FAIR
HIS VOICE ESCAPES IN A HIGH TRILL
AND HE GOES

91

Colorful balloons! Today
only today
a dozen
a doz————————en for a quarter!
For a quarter.

And the tune is terribly
familiar.

WITH EYES WIDE OPEN

92

Angels angels of heaven
your hearts hearts of white chalk your minds of granite
don't die of self-love. If there is ever
a time for angels please crown his glory
in a crown of fire

who is this man! Waving his flowering balloons
like a king who spreads out his awning
he gets up. Turns—
the sandy wind seems to split to give
way to the chariot of his voice struggling with its consonants:

A STRUGGLE FULL OF COMPASSION
BETWEEN THE MEMORY AND ITS REPRESSION

D – A – M – B – A – M   (He spells)

Dam—bam   (Pronounces. Remembers.)

My son   (Laughs or

    cries)

Your inheritance

not your rest

A Returned Gate:
In Spite of All This Something Does Not
Let Go

HE

93

He stayed behind me on the dunes
please open your door, open it for him, sister.
Oh, my disbelieving body! Can there
be spring without the danger?
Love gives up its last breath
in order to live. Those who love
and don't want to escape, who love
and couldn't forgive.

You'll win, sister. My heavy hands
are lifted.

AND I

94

No, my dear. In the name of all these days, no!
Don't hand me over to a mute wall
embalmed in the sounds of words—
I am the threshold of your holidays.
I am the candles in your forgotten
candlesticks. I am not to be blamed
if I lie empty at the shore of your body
and at the shore of your body I open,
a sea, in a set time.

Make me grow, my love, in soil as naked

as it was created.

Twelfth Gate:
A Farewell Song and Words
from the Drunk Who Embraces an Empty Bottle
Like a Guitar

95

The best woman, young man, is a desired
woman. The best way, my friend,
leads to a sea to a desert
to an odor of salt and rain an odor of stone scorched by the sun
a taste of ore of iron and blood
to a place from which there is no way
except for the ones who go, my boy.

Be thirsty, brother,
be thirsty. Only the one who is thirsty
has enough

and more than enough.

IT'S LATE

96

Naked soil is the way to my beloved.
I come to her like someone coming to a tryst.
I quietly try to rebuild
a city, transparent. To sail confused houses
in two-way streets. To give them back
their faces, to arrange
rotating crops, to let the sea
break through into the small square
rooms and wash the frost flowers
and sand stripes alternately from the windows
like an old-fashioned devoted servant. Already

there is a road.
A road sign.
It's really possible to go. I will only hang
my hat on the acacia branch
to sway, I will set
my eye in the new streetlights so they will not close
in difficult moments. In the neck of the weather vane
I have already tied my tie
with the pure gold pin
I inherited from my father. I will spread
my shirt before the first policeman's
dog who will come on time

running in front of his master. And my shoes
I will leave my shoes—
for the cat
until a better story will be found
for the city children
and you
only you, my little sister, will I take with me
on my back. To carry you beyond
my naked plot of soil.

In a dozen scenes   show me   hidden canopies
within canopies   and I asked the elders   what
is it and they said mysterious   and I asked
birds going south   what is it that you see
and they said to me   abyss within abyss   and
I did not insist   and I called   my friends
should I persist   no voice divine
no king to find

There is a hive for bees for snakes a season
a way for eagles a map for the sea and none
for me   for dreams recurring   no meaning no
reason   only the curse   and
whoever yearns to read will come   I look
above me   a sea of silence   I speak to
myself   I speak and speak   I'll return
I'll return here   alive

APPENDIX: A Letter from Abba Kovner

TEXTUAL NOTES

Appendix

A Letter from Abba Kovner
Regarding the Difficult Translation of Poem 41 in
My Little Sister

At first thought, a simple letter. And at the end,
a strange story. Dedicated to the bridesmaids of
my sister: Shirley Kaufman and Nurit Orchan.

*

My father, of blessed memory, had a beautiful voice. He led the prayers. My father was proud when the leaders of the community used to surround him after the *Musaf* [the additional service on the Sabbath], praise him and say: "Bravo, Rabbi Israel, bravo!"

Maybe, even then, I already said to myself, in my heart, that I would have a voice.

My father was not a cantor, and wasn't even observant. In the *yeshiva* [school for advanced study of the Talmud] where he studied, he was reared as a genius. And eventually he was snared by the "Enlightenment" and became far removed from strict observance. But the chanting of the prayers, and especially the *piyutim* [hymns]—*piyutim* of the Sabbath and of holidays—came from his mouth with extra sweetness.

So he was standing near the window as it turned dark, the Sabbath was almost over, and he, with his hands at his back, was singing to himself "*Melavey Malka*" [a hymn for the closing of the Sabbath]. At this hour, he seemed to me someone who is talking to a distant land. I was too little to understand that this land was already gone.

*

One *piyut* my father sang in a special way. It was one of the songs of the Sabbath, which in our generation people don't often sing. And it opens with the words: "How beautiful you are and how pleasant you are among pleasures, you, Sabbath, the eve of sweet sadness." Written by Mordechai ben Itzhak in the twelfth century, it compares the people of Israel to the legendary river Sambatyon, which also rests from its turmoil only on the Sabbath. The time for this *piyut* is on Friday night, and the melody of this *piyut* is especially haunting.

My father did not sing it like the rest of the Jews. When he began the words, "*Ma yafit* [how beautiful]," something which tore the heart was in his voice.

But very rarely were we privileged to hear the song from his mouth, and always when he was unaware. When we were at the Sabbath table, we begged him to sing it to us. But he would answer with a wave of the hand, like driving a bad fly away from him, and then angry silence.

*

At one Sabbath dinner, he went far with his singing. At the beginning, we sang with him, and then he clasped his fingers over his eyebrows and began to sing to himself. Suddenly he began this *piyut*.

Everyone was silent for some reason, and only I continued along with him in a thin voice. After a minute or two, he noticed it; he stopped and said gravely: "Son, you will *not* sing *this!*" Spoke and looked at me in a strange way.

Clearly he saw my consternation. And also the tears which gathered in my eyes from the insult. He rubbed his hands together while he thought it over, and he said:

*

"I was a child almost your age when I accompanied my grand-father, of blessed memory, during a summer vacation on his travels to the courts of the Polish landowners. He was accepted by the Polish landlords as a decent and honest salesman for ornaments and precious stones. And he made his living from them. One landlord liked my grandfather especially. I saw with my own eyes how this Pole sat my grandfather at their dinner table, set with the prohibited [not kosher] best, and ordered him to sing to him 'Ma Yafit.'

"Grandfather had a wonderful voice, trilling and chanting. His white beard swayed while he sang, like wheat before the morning breeze. The Pole, his sons and his sons' sons and all their wives were at this moment deep in pork fat, digging with their fingers into the bowl in front of them, and only rolled back fat eyes in the Jew's direction with vulgar pleasure.

"Grandfather sang, and I cried."

*

That's how I was first introduced to the tragic transformation of the *piyut*. But I was probably rebellious in my mother's womb. The evening when my father stopped the singing on account of me, not understanding him, I went to my room. And when I paced from wall to wall, I sang out of the fullness of my throat, again and again, "*Ma yafit* . . ." But alas, I had no voice. When I repeated the song the fifth or sixth time, it was more like a cavalry march than a Sabbath *piyut*.

In the days when I was already a leader in Hashomer Hatzair (a Zionist youth organization), spending nights like days around the campfire with my group, when singing was like a prayer in our mouths, how many agonies of soul and body I suffered when my voice sailed out from the choir and was heard in solo! Only false notes and disaster. Humiliation and disaster!

*

I was thirteen, less one day, when I vowed the only vow in my life. I had heard from my mother, of blessed memory, that the voice of a child, like food cooked in a pot, needs to be cooked until a sort of mutation takes place. And it wouldn't be many days after Bar Mitzvah that I would have, with God's help, a voice of my own.

The day before I was called to the Torah, right after the morn-
ing prayers, I vowed my vow. And I engraved it on paper like
parchment (I oiled the paper with clear olive oil and tied it with
a red ribbon). In these words: "My God, If you will grant me a
pleasing voice, I am ready to give you five years of my life." Ex-
cited, I signed my full name and kept my secret.

I did not know what a strange trader God is, and how cruel is
His authority. My best five years fell prey to the devil, as it is
known. But to this day, I did not get a pleasing voice in return.

*

Of all the prayer books, I most loved the *maḥzor*, which is a
collection separate from the usual prayer book, because of the
many *piyutim* for the Days of Awe. From the day I became in-
volved in reading and prayer, the passages of the *piyut* in it worked
a special magic on me, because of their interpretation, hidden
from my understanding, or because of their structure. In the
maḥzor of Pesach, Shavuot, and Succot [holidays], which was avail-
able in my father's home, published by the Brothers and the
Widow Rom, most of the *piyutim* were written in ornamental let-
ters, not like the giant letters of the *kiddush* [sanctification] for
the New Moon, and not like the usual prayers which have thin
and hasty letters that the tongue squeezes like hot noodles. Those
were respectable letters with character and faces. Truly, faces!
Each of them had a style and a face of its own—one with a serious
face, one with a happy face. Those dotted letters looking at you
with lighted eyes, and others leaning like pious women with eyes
closed. And all in all, their stance, confident. Among them, like a
poet in the midst of corpulent bodies, bewildered, by himself,
stood a dreaming *"vav"* [the narrowest letter in the Hebrew alpha-
bet], hardpressed and humble, but in spite of it, repeating its
appearance now in the middle, now at the end of the line, as if it
would be impossible to make an orderly prayer without it.

*

Unlike the litany in the Christian liturgy, which is mostly done by the leader of the prayers with the congregation responding, the essentials of the Hebrew *piyut* are recited by the congregation and the least parts by the leader. And thus they are written in the book. Wide, wide lines, close to each other, big ones and small ones, ornate and modest. And there is almost no separation between them. Standing crowded, kneeling at intervals, like the people of Israel on a pilgrimage to Jerusalem. And here they stood in the Temple court, joyous, and ready for the Day of Judgment.

When I learned the history of the *piyut*, I saw that the first composers only composed their *piyutim* to decorate and beautify the body of the prayers. And the composers who came after, because in their generation preaching in matters of Law was prohibited by the rulers, made the *piyut* substitute for the preaching. And furthermore, these *piyutim* were nothing but rhymed rhetoric, minor to the main theme.

I did not like the interpretations by which the *piyut* was explained by linguists and researchers. In these days of my childhood, with plenty of knowledge before knowledge, I did not understand the explanation regarding the texts that many words in the *piyut* are difficult, and they have strange combinations. What I perceived from them, I did not perceive from the strength of the hidden allegory in the stories of the *Agada*, but from the sound of the language and the rhythm of the song. This is what descended on my memory like the tapping of the first rain on listening earth.

*

And like this, they came back to me after twenty or thirty years.

It's true that many of them are in my poems, not as they are, but like something which happens only once and leaves its flavor and aroma for years. No. Not for the sake of ornamentation, and not as a sort of artifice did they come into my poems. But—how shall I say it—like windows. Maybe like small windows cut in a prison wall. Through them comes a small light and through them is reflected, near, yet unattainable, another world, real and imagined.

When I wrote chapter 40 of *My Little Sister*, and I arrived at the last lines of the page, I became confused. As if land were dropping away under my feet. It is not that I did not know how I wanted to continue or where I was going. Simply, I didn't know how to take the *next* step.

Probably you have hiked in the mountains. Everyone who climbs high mountains assumes that every time he climbs a cliff, a chasm will appear next. Like the years of the mountain, so the days of the chasm. Not so in our Negev, or in the Judean desert which is the desert of the Jews. It is possible that your feet will walk on the plain for an hour, ten hours, confidently in the sand which is somewhat yielding. And its foundation is solid, and the earth behind you and before you is even and spread out. And all the way, the plain. But suddenly everything is cut off. And at your feet, a real chasm. Narrow, dark and long. And according to the map, and according to the logic, there is no chasm here. Only yesterday, there was a clear path here continuing unbroken. But the day before yesterday, somewhere, a terrible flood fell, and the earth ripped open at once as if from a murderer's knife. And there is no way to cross. Unless a rope will be thrown from the other side.

*

Chapter 41 was lying in front of me, white and empty, and the end of the rope was not in my hand. And my hands were over my eyes:

> the shorn head of my sister
> breaks out of a wall. . . .

She stands on the other side and does not hear me, does not understand my language. My God! There must be a language which will make a bridge between us. A language of the living which the dead will also hear and understand.

And then I hear the voice of the syllables like drops of rain

which fall on a hot tin roof: *ridudi . . . midadi . . . gdudi . . . kitvi
. . . matfi . . . dodi . . . litsvi . . . li . . . bemar li . . .*
 I didn't know how they came to me. And I didn't ask at this time
or this hour about their origins. Like a woman beaten by a dry
season who comes hesitantly toward the first rain, I collected the
drops in a small bowl.
 Still I remember the magic sound of the words while they fell.
Like the weeping of many violins.

ABBA KOVNER
Translated from the Hebrew
by Shirley Kaufman with Nurit Orchan

Textual Notes

My Little Sister

P. 20, l. 10

My fragile sister. The "little sister" of the title, an allusion to Song of Songs 8:8, is connected here through an allusive pun to the sister-bride invoked through the Song of Songs. The Hebrew word *kala* can mean "slight," "quick," "blithe," and, in a different spelling, it means "bride." Combining the two meanings in English translation, the translators chose "fragile."

P. 48, l. 1

Oh one who commanded us. A fragmentary echo of the formula used in the traditional benediction recited before carrying out a divine commandment.

P. 49, ll. 8–9, l. 15

Kosher chicken soup . . . dumplings. It was the custom among Eastern European Jews for bride and groom to share a bowl of clear chicken broth after the marriage ceremony. The *ḥallah,* or twisted loaf of Sabbath bread, was part of the festive wedding meal.

P. 59, ll. 4–5

Behold you / are consecrated. Part of the formula recited by the groom to the bride during the marriage ceremony: "Behold you are consecrated unto me with this ring according to the law of Moses and Israel." The previous line also alluded to a wedding, being a verbatim quotation from Song of Songs 8:8, the verse that introduces the little sister who is to be married.

P. 62, l. 1

Behold you. The truncated beginning of the marriage ceremony formula, made clear by the allusion in the third line to the traditional bridal canopy under which the ceremony is conducted.

P. 64

The Hebrew here imitates the peculiar style of the medieval *piyut,* or liturgical poem, with its exaggerated use of internal rhyme, alliteration, wordplay, and its densely allusive quality (see the Appendix for Kovner's explanation). The key allusion here, made clear in the Hebrew through the insistence on the word *dodi,* "my love," is to the Song of Songs. In this section the translation has concentrated more on retaining the songlike quality than on the exact literal meaning.

P. 69, l. 3

A candle for the saving of her soul. An allusion to the traditional Jewish practice in which the mourner, during the first week of bereavement or on the anniversary of a death, lights a candle for the "saving" or ascent of the departed soul.

P. 69, l. 11

Eight years. In the Hebrew they are specified, 1940 to 1948.

P. 71, ll. 9–10

Imi / imi. Hebrew: "my mother, my mother," echoing the "with me" *(imi)* of the previous line. The repeated syllables may be, among other things, a reversal of an expected, "And say with me / amen, amen."

A Parting from the South

P. 77, l. 10

Azekah. A place bordering the northern Negev in Israel, the area in which the Givati Brigade ended the battle in the south during the Israeli War of Independence. Azekah is often mentioned in the Bible in connection with the wars of Israel (i.e., Josh. 10:10–11).

P. 77, l. 22

Grar. A city and region in the Negev in which Abraham and Isaac dwelled (Genesis 20 and 26). Grar was located on the way to Egypt.

P. 77, l. 23

Kedar. An Arab tribe, mentioned in the Bible, whose members were described as "mighty men" (Isa. 21:17).

P. 81

Radio silence. In the original Hebrew text Abba Kovner wrote the following note: "When a fighting unit used to leave for the battlefield with its commander and all the last-minute instructions were given in writing, by mouth, and by loudspeaker, and when all the allocated equipment was assigned and nothing was left to add to the planning of the mission, nothing to change, and the unit dispersed to face the enemy, the commander used to transmit to head-quarters his last wish before the battle: let this hour be an hour of *radio silence*, silence in the field, silence between a man and his leader, silence be-tween hill and hill. And the ear is not open to the radio receiver, but to the sound of what will happen, fated, and hidden in what is to come."

P. 81, l. 2

Dambam. In the notes to the Hebrew edition, the author comments: "I did not know the man; I only heard his name during those nights, from far away, and its sound penetrated to me, strange and exciting. The man was killed. And I was left with only the rhythm of this name—Dambam." Dambam does not exist as a Hebrew proper name.

P. 86, l. 4

Doorpost. The *mezuza*, translated here as "doorpost," is the distinctive mark of the Jewish home. It contains a small roll of parchment with a sacred text, and it is fixed on the entrance to houses and on the gates of cities (Deut. 6:4–9; 11:13–21). The dog tag becomes a substitute for the *mezuza*.

P. 87, l. 1

Ḥirbet Fatatah. An Arab stronghold bordering the northern Negev and locked on its north side by two towns—Kharatiya and Ḥata.

A Canopy in the Desert

P. 97, l. 13

Five scrolls. Books grouped together in the Bible at the time of its canoniza-tion, forming a distinct unit (Song of Songs, Ruth, Lamentations, Ecclesiastes, Esther), which were traditionally published with twelve different commen-taries surrounding them.

P. 99, l. 2

Avdat. An ancient city south of Beersheba, recently rediscovered and recon-structed through archaeological excavations. Avdat has Nabatean, Roman, and Byzantine ruins from the first to the seventh centuries.

P. 100, l. 2

Mount Eldad. A mountain located northeast of Avdat.

[219]

P. 101, l. 7

Bsor. A river valley (wadi) and a region in the Negev.

P. 102

Grar. See note, p. 218.

P. 107, l. 3

600,000. See the reference to the 600,000 Hebrew slaves in the Introduction, page xxiii.

P. 107, l. 8

A fault. The Hebrew word here, *dayka,* has been translated into a more widely known geologic term, *fault.* Igneous material intrudes into fissures in the earth's surface to create "dikes." A "fault" is a fissure along which there has been a notable displacement.

P. 123, ll. 13–14

Cities / of refuge. The reference is to "the six cities of refuge where you shall permit the manslayer to flee" (Num. 35:6). The man who fled there was protected from the tribal law of blood revenge so that he might receive a trial.

P. 132, l. 8

Ofir. Mentioned in the Bible as the land of gold (i.e., 1 Kings 9:28). Its exact location is doubtful, though it was believed to be somewhere south of the land of Israel.

P. 136, l. 13

Arbor Day. The Jewish holiday Tu B'Shevat (the fifteenth day of the month of Shevat in the Hebrew calendar) is mentioned in the Mishna (Talmud) as the new year of the trees. In this century it has gained new meaning as Arbor Day, observed by the planting of trees and reforestation in the land of Israel.

P. 139, l. 9

Jebel Libni. A mountain in the northeastern part of the Sinai peninsula.

P. 139, l. 9

Valley of Nakhl. Located in the west-central section of the Sinai peninsula.

P. 145, l. 2

Wheatgroats. Bulgar wheat, a common Arab food.

P. 147, l. 2

Waladi. Arabic, meaning "my son."

P. 153, l. 1

Jiddi Pass. Located north of Jebel Libni in the Sinai peninsula. Bloody battles took place there.

P. 156

St. Catherine's Monastery. Located in the mountainous south central region of Sinai, this Greek Orthodox monastery, more than a thousand years old, is set at the base of Mount Sinai, believed to be the mountain where Moses received the Ten Commandments.

The Mountain of Mountains. A literal translation of the Hebrew name for Mount Sinai where Moses received the Law.

P. 157

Unpronounced Vowels. The Hebrew title for this section is four Hebrew letters: Alef, He, Vav, Yod. These letters, which are used today only as vowels and whose pronunciation has changed, had, in ancient times, a pronunciation of their own. They are referred to as "mothers of reading" in Hebrew, and the eleventh-century Spanish-Jewish poet Yehuda Halevi called them "mothers of the Torah and its roots." The poet hints here that these unclear kernels of the language are transmitted from as far as a lost planet. And they are filled with content and meaning, although we can no longer decipher them.

P. 161

The Mitla Pass. Located in the center of the Sinai peninsula, north of the Suez Canal, this narrow defile, stretching for miles, figured prominently in the Arab-Israeli wars of 1956 and 1967.

P. 162, l. 3

A black girl. The story of "the Cushite woman" whom Moses married is found in Num. 12:1. *Cushite* is the Hebrew, translated here as *black.*

P. 170, l. 12

Law. The Hebrew refers to the Law of the Torah (the first five books of the Bible), which contains the central core of Jewish law.

P. 176, l. 6

Marriage contract. The Hebrew word is *ketuba,* meaning "written document," the marriage contract containing the mutual obligations between husband and wife prerequisite to marriage.

P. 183, l. 8

Rabbi Nathan. From "Avot De-Rabbi Nathan," the Hebrew for "The Fathers

According to Rabbi Nathan," one of the extracanonical minor tractates of the Talmud. This part of the Talmud is traditionally printed in very small characters; hence its reading is technically difficult.

P. 185, l. 1

The glass shattered. A reference to Jewish wedding ceremony tradition, which includes the breaking of a glass in memory of the destruction of the Temple in Jerusalem.

P. 186, l. 9

The horns of the altar. These were projections resembling horns at the four corners of an altar (Exod. 29:12). An altar was sacred; a person touching it was not supposed to be slain (1 Kings 1:50).

P. 187, l. 8

Chosen boy. The Hebrew here is *shats,* an abbreviation for *Sheliaḥ Tsibur,* which means, literally, "the messenger of the congregation." It applies to the person leading the congregation in prayer.

P. 189, l. 15

Behold you. See note, p. 217.

P. 191

Wadi of Paran. Located in the southern part of the Sinai peninsula.

P. 193, ll. 8–15

This is Ḥirbet Fatatah! . . . This is a quotation from the poem "Voices from the Hill" in *A Parting from the South* (see p. 87). It evokes the memory of the War of Independence.

PITT POETRY SERIES

James Den Boer, *Learning the Way*
    (1967 U.S. Award of the International Poetry Forum)
James Den Boer, *Trying to Come Apart*
Jon Anderson, *Looking for Jonathan*
Jon Anderson, *Death & Friends*
John Engels, *The Homer Mitchell Place*
Samuel Hazo, *Blood Rights*
Samuel Hazo, *Once for the Last Bandit: New and Previous Poems*
David P. Young, *Sweating Out the Winter*
    (1968 U.S. Award of the International Poetry Forum)
Fazıl Hüsnü Dağlarca, *Selected Poems*
    (International Poetry Forum Selection translated from the Turkish)
Jack Anderson, *The Invention of New Jersey*
Gary Gildner, *First Practice*
Gary Gildner, *Digging for Indians*
David Steingass, *Body Compass*
Shirley Kaufman, *The Floor Keeps Turning*
    (1969 U.S. Award of the International Poetry Forum)
Michael S. Harper, *Dear John, Dear Coltrane*
Michael S. Harper, *Song: I Want a Witness*
Ed Roberson, *When Thy King Is A Boy*
Gerald W. Barrax, *Another Kind of Rain*
Abbie Huston Evans, *Collected Poems*
Richard Shelton, *The Tattooed Desert*
    (1970 U.S. Award of the International Poetry Forum)
Richard Shelton, *Of All the Dirty Words*
Adonis, *The Blood of Adonis*
    (International Poetry Forum Selection translated from the Arabic)
Norman Dubie, *Alehouse Sonnets*
Larry Levis, *Wrecking Crew*
    (1971 U.S. Award of the International Poetry Forum)
Tomas Tranströmer, *Windows & Stones: Selected Poems*
    (International Poetry Forum Selection translated from the Swedish)
Abba Kovner, *A Canopy in the Desert: Selected Poems*
    (International Poetry Forum Selection translated from the Hebrew)
Marc Weber, *48 Small Poems*
    (1972 U.S. Award of the International Poetry Forum)
Belle Randall, *101 Different Ways of Playing Solitaire and Other Poems*

This book was set in Linotype Baskerville types and printed by letterpress by the Heritage Printers, Inc. The paper is Warren's Olde Style Wove, an acid-free sheet calculated to remain stable for 300 years. The design is by Gary Gore.